Ema Earns
Her Ears

Ema Earns Her Ears

My Secret Walt Disney World
Cast Member Diary

EARNING YOUR EARS: VOLUME TWO

Ema Hutton

Theme Park Press

Theme Park Press publishes its books in a variety of print and electronic formats. Some content that appears in one format may not appear in another.

Editor: Bob McLain
Layout: Artisanal Text

ISBN 978-1-941500-25-5
Printed in the United States of America

Theme Park Press | **www.ThemeParkPress.com**
Address queries to bob@themeparkpress.com

In memory of my granddad who passed away before he could hear any of my Disney stories, and my nana, who passed away during my second program, but who saw pictures and heard of stories before she went to join my granddad.

Contents

Introduction

I remember from a very young age dressing up in a homemade, golden Belle gown, or as Pocahontas complete with long black wig. My playroom was covered from floor to ceiling with Disney characters, including a scene of Peter Pan chasing his shadow around the ceiling light that my mum had painted. I loved my childhood.

I remember my first trip to Disney World, and it's complete with a quote that my dad will never let me forget. He asked me, on camera, where we were, to which I replied enthusiastically: *"DISNEY!"* We weren't a family that would return to the "Happiest Place on Earth" every year, and I'm glad, because each visit was special, and not just an annual pilgrimage that we had to take. My family worked hard to afford these trips. Even now, I still get excited over a prospect of a trip to Disney World. My life revolved around watching a new Disney film on VHS, while being surrounded by my mountains of Disney character plush toys, and being able to visit the place where these characters seemed to exist made it all real, at least to a child, and I suppose to a few adults, as well.

As a kid, I was always Disney orientated; I don't really know how or why I became this way, but when I reached age where I realized that the true magic of Disney was made by people like myself, I decided that one day I wanted to make that magic, too. I wanted to become a Disney cast member.

In December 2008, we were on a holiday in Disney World. I remember engaging in conversation with a cast member working on front desk at the Pop Century resort while we were checking in. I told her that I wanted to work here, and that I wanted to make magic. Although she was trying to go through the process of explaining to my parents everything they needed to know, from transportation and Disney park hours to the food court, she did spend some time at the end of our check in and gave me a number for Casting. I was over the moon.

But little did I, and little did that cast member, realize that to be able to work in Florida, as an International, I would need a working VISA, and Disney wouldn't just hand one over to me. I never rang Casting when I was there, and thinking back, I don't really know why, but I kept the piece of paper, and still to this day I can tell you it's in a cardboard, pin-striped shoe box under my bed. I've kept hold of it like a dream.

Even though I've now worked for Disney, and seen what it's like from behind the curtain, Disney is still a huge part of who I am, even though my childish notions of princesses and characters and magic have given way to their sometimes harsh reality. Every little girl may dream to one day grow up to be a Disney princess, and I had those dreams, but at some point they changed to dreams of becoming a Disney cast member.

And you know what? My dreams came true.

This book is about what happened next.

PART ONE
Housekeeping

My first program took me on an up and down journey in the world of housekeeping at Walt Disney World, starting May 6, 2012, and ending on August 3.

As they say, "For every up, there is a down, that's what makes the world go round." I seemed to get more than my fair share of lows, but I always remained positive and tried to find the good in every situation.

CHAPTER ONE

Application

If we are to start right at the very beginning, where we should, I have to take you back to November 2009. I was traveling with my dad to the University of Chester in England for an open day event. I was applying for a combined degree in drama and events management, and I wanted to attend a presentation put on by the Events Management Department. Since I knew next to nothing about events management, this presentation was a big deal for me.

As I sat outside the seminar room, along came a man who introduced himself in a warm, friendly voice as Martin Metcalfe. Little did I know that this man, a complete stranger, was about to deliver some information that would change my life. Within five minutes into the presentation, I knew that events managements would be right for me, and I was completely sold on taking Mr. Metcalfe's course. Then, the presentation slide changed, and there was a picture of Mickey Mouse standing in front of Cinderella Castle on Main Street, U.S.A., in Walt Disney World. My mind froze; I fixated upon that image. I listened intently as Metcalfe explained about the Disney College Program and the many students from the University of Chester who had enrolled and had enjoyed the experience immensely.

Now come with me to September 2010. I had packed up my room at home and bundled all of my books and electronics into the car, along with all manner of odds and ends that I couldn't leave behind. Once again, my dad and I set out on the two-hour drive to Chester, where I would be attending classes and moving into an all-girls dorm house.

First Interview

And now we'll jump forward one more time, to October 2011. I was attending a work-based learning lecture on how boring the next six weeks of my life will be. But I knew that things were about to change, since finally it was time for me to apply to the Disney College Program, as I had planned to do since first setting foot in the University of Chester. Not only would I work at Disney World, if accepted, but the experience would earn me credits toward my degree. Perfect!

Except for one problem: I hadn't been told to sign up for an interview or been told to attend the presentation.

My heart sunk. I felt that I had missed my chance and was able to hold back the tears only because I didn't want others to see me cry. I found the room where members of Disney's UK recruitment company were conducting interviews, and I stood outside the door for 30 minutes in hopes that someone would notice me and invite me inside. Other students asked me if I was here for the interview, too, and without even thinking I said "yes". As soon as the words left my mouth, I felt guilty about the lie; I felt like I was jinxing an opportunity that I hadn't even been given yet.

I heard chairs moving and lots of talking and all of a sudden the door opened. I saw a lot of people, all dressed similar to me, then I saw a man thanking people for coming. His black polo shirt had the recruiting company's logo embroidered on it, and I knew he was the man I had to see.

By now, the hall was packed with students who were scheduled for this group interview slot. I couldn't bluff my way in, and so I steeled myself for the embarrassment of having to ask the man if he could add me to a later group. I just hoped the girl I had lied to moments ago didn't overhear! I walked quickly toward the man at the door, knowing I might have to fight for my dream. He stood patiently as I explained my situation, and then he let me walk straight into the interview. If only it all had went so smoothly...

The room that now was full of people, maybe 20–30 in all, and some of them were wearing three-piece suits. Most were dressed at least semi-professionally. I, on the other hand, was wearing a pair of faded blue jeans, brown boots, and a bright pink university hoodie.

Could it get any worse? Yes.

I sat down in the only seat left, at the front next to the two recruiters. I watched the other candidates pull out their resumes and photographs and cover letters. I had none of these things. I began to regret talking my way into this interview. But the Disney gods must have been smiling upon me, because after a recruiter chatted briefly with me, she agreed to let me email her the necessary documents as soon as I got back home. With renewed hope, I decided to give this my best shot.

Still, I felt an insane amount of pressure and overwhelmed by the number of students (just from my university alone) competing against me for the limited number of positions available. I also felt unprepared and inadequate. And the worse did, in fact, happen: I made a complete and utter fool of myself, which really is no different than what I do during any other day in my life, but the one time when I needed to be sensible and prove my worth, I did one of the silliest things, ever.

As I sat there, in front of all the other candidates, I answered the questions posed to me with structured and detailed responses. I began to convince myself that the recruiters liked what I was telling them; I read into their tight smiles what I imagined was their excitement at finding me such a perfect candidate. I forgot that the girl next to me, poised and confident, was wearing her best suit in stark comparison to my hoodie and jeans. I was sure that I was doing well enough to be called back for the all-important second interview.

The next question sent around the horse-shoe shaped table for everyone to answer was, "Which character best describes you, and why?"

The other students were offering carefully rehearsed, falsely profound, and often just plain pretentious answers, and clearly none of what they were saying was true. One girl, for example, said: "I'm like Ariel—you know, from *The Little Mermaid*." (Stupid, really, as if anyone in that room didn't know what film Ariel was from, and if they didn't know, they should have gotten up and left then.) The girl continued: "I think she best describes me because I've always felt like I don't fit in anywhere, and I don't belong, and I really feel like I want to be part of Disney's world as much as Ariel wanted to walk on land." I was hoping that the recruiters would ask her if she was willing to give up her rather annoying voice to be part of that world, but of course in real life such perfect replies never happen.

But now it's coming up to my turn. I haven't decided yet what to say. Should I try the profound approach, or should I just go with "I'm like Belle because I've grown up watching *Beauty and the Beast* and feel I have a real connection to her." That might not win me the prize, but it wouldn't disqualify me, either. Then I think,, I'm nothing like Belle, I'm strange, but not her kind of strange, my dad is kind of crazy, but again not that crazy, and I really don't like reading that much, at least not read the same book over and over.

When it came turn, I panicked. Belle flew from my mind. I said: "I think Russell from *Up* best describes me". Despite the funny looks and titters, I pressed on. "It's not because my elbow and knees hurt, or because I'm secretly a Boy Scout in a hunt to find someone elderly I can assist, but it's because I love adventures, and all things new, people and places." The titters had stopped, and I saw from the corner of my eye some guy nodding his head in agreement. The recruiters were jotting down notes. It was a great answer, and I really should have stopped there. But I didn't.

"Also, I do the best Russell impression."

The guy stopped nodding his head, and the recruiters stopped taking notes. I should have noticed that and smiled sweetly. Instead, with every ounce of confidence and energy I could muster, I yelled: *"The wilderness must be explored, ka ka, RARRRRRR!"*

If this wasn't embarrassing enough, there were physical movements that went along with the words, and if you've seen the film you'll understand why I laugh so much now about what I did. If you haven't seen the film, I won't spoil it for you—just search on YouTube for "the wilderness must be explored".

Whether it was my amazing, yet embarrassing, impression of Russell, or that I actually gave some good answers, or maybe because they just liked me, despite the missing paperwork and all the other things I'd done wrong, I got the second interview. I swore that I wouldn't go into that interview as unprepared as I'd gone into the first.

Second Interview

This is the really fun part of the process, because you're able to let your personality shine through and not have to suffer through generic questions. Disney wants to get to know you, and they genuinely do, and they will remember you. Don't think that they see so many people that no matter what you say you'll just be a number, because that is not true at all. Disney wants to hire the right people, the best people, and so they spend enough time with candidates to ensure that they don't make any mistakes.

It was November 11, 2011, the day of my second interview for my first Disney College Program. Two Disney casting recruiters came to my university from Walt Disney World. The UK recruiters introduced them to us as Jill and Mike. I had never seen people before with so much energy and who smiled as much as they did. It intimidated me, in a way, but it also motivated me to do my absolute best.

Jill and Mike were in love with England and our accents; they even did a little bit where they tried out their own English accent (which wasn't too bad, except that it was the same stereotypical British accent that all Americans think we have). We watched the usual upbeat presentations and played a quiz game with Disney trivia questions about the parks, TV shows, films, and characters. We were then given an interview slot and sent on our way until it was our turn to come back to see the Disney recruiters. I lived just down the road from the university, so I used this time to go home, calm my nerves, and have some lunch, which I remember was a cheese and ham toasty, though I only nibbled at the edges before it made me feel sick. I ended up watching some TV to take my mind off the interview, and then, feeling that I should be doing even more to prepare, I went online to some of the Disney College Program forum and looked up answers to the common questions that candidates were asked. They hadn't changed since the last time I looked them up.

Finally, the time came. I checked through my paperwork my last time, checked my appearance in the mirror, and off I went back to university.

I had a lovely partner who also studied events management but was a year below me, and while we were going over our paperwork the recruiters encouraged us to chat and get to know each other beforehand. This came in handy, because we could discuss answers between ourselves rather than the recruiter directing the same question to each of us in turn.

Although we each got to answer every question, it still felt like a competition. We were asked about our previous work experience; I had helped out in my parent's tearoom, while my interview partner had run events at a pub, taken a full course load at university, and maintained a 100% attendance record. I began to feel like I might have to pull out another Russell impression.

We were also asked about our role preferences. I had ticked every role possible in the hope that I would be accepted for something, anything, although I did express my passion for drama and had made performer my number one choice. When the recruiter saw that, he asked for my height. I told him, and he immediately told me that it put me in the "dead height" category and then moved on to extol the virtues of quick service food and beverage roles, and would I enjoy working at an insanely busy location during the hot, crowded summer months. I brought up my previous experience as a waitress, and of course my interview partner then brought up hers, which was far superior to mine. The positive vibes I had felt from the recruiter at the start of the interview had now completely vanished.

Even before I walked out the door, I was forcing myself to accept that I'd be staying in England.

CHAPTER TWO

Acceptance

Ever since the disastrous (at least that's how I saw it) second interview, I'd been downplaying the college program and soon people knew not to discuss it with me.

It was November 29, the day after my dad's birthday and the start of my "reading week", so I was able to go home and spend time with my family. Although I was still depressed, I was enjoying doing the usual "bits and bobs" shopping with my parents. My mum had darted across the road in front of busy traffic, leaving my dad and myself on the other side waiting for a safe opportunity to cross. As we stood there, my phone vibrated in my pocket. One vibration, and that means email. I was waiting for Disney's decision, which they'd send me by email, but after so many days had passed, my heart no longer raced quite as much when I got new email.

But this time was different: email from Disney International Recruitment! I read it once, then read it a second time. I looked up to see my mum waiting across the road. I shouted to her—and to everyone else within earshot:

I HAVE BEEN ACCEPTED TO WORK AT DISNEY WORLD!

I didn't even care that I had gotten Housekeeping, a role at the bottom of my priority list. I was going to be a Disney Cast Member. From that moment on, it was all about booking, planning, and excitement.

Months pass. It's March 4, 2012 (you are probably thinking, "wow, she is really good with dates," but honestly there are only a few dates that stick in my head, and all the rest are logged online in one of my many notebooks and diaries, and in the journal that I kept at Disney and which became the basis for this book). Also, since I'd be getting credit for my work experience at Disney World, I had to keep notes while I was there and then write a briefing paper to submit to the university upon my return. So documenting every little thing was already second nature.

Now that it had finally sunk in that I was going to work at Disney World, I began searching the internet for hours on end looking for information about what to expect. There was plenty of material for the regular college program, but not so much for the *international* college program. I decided to set up my own blog to write about it. On April 6, I posted an update creatively entitled "Update". So many of the other Disney college program blogs I'd read were titling each post with Disney movie quotes that fitted what they were about to say, but for some reason, my creative side was holding back. I would have laughed at anyone who told me back then that in two years I'd be writing a book on my experience.

In addition to the blog, I decided to also keep a handwritten journal with the intent to submit it as an appendix to my university assessment. I found that I preferred it over the blog. My first entry, dated April 18, 2012, began in plain black ink with, "The start to my Disney journey...18 days to go." I continued to write in the notebook, keeping track of my preparations and expectations, and even including multiple quotes from *Finding Nemo*—each in a different colored felt-tip pen, of course.

The first week after being accepted, I started googling "cute summer clothes" and pricing denim shorts and sunglasses. I wanted to buy everything straight away and begin to pack. I wrote my first to-do list before I even knew precisely what I'd have to do, but I took my best shot at it, and came up with the obvious:

- Book flights
- Make friends with people on my flight
- Research Disney housing and surrounding area
- Look at more Disney College Program blogs
- Buy shorts and sunglasses
- Search for vlogs on "Housekeeping"
- Make a bucket list

Looking back, I see how naïve it was of me to think that all I had to do was book a flight and show up at the gates to Disney World, where all would be taken care of. There were many, many more elements to pre-Disney preparations that never crossed my mind. Someone had told me about getting a student work visa during one of the presentations, but the excitement of being accepted by Disney made me forget such practical matters, and so I focused on making friends and making bucket lists instead of researching the visa interview process.

Reading blogs written by former Disney College Program participants was my biggest weakness; all I wanted to do was read new posts, watch YouTube videos, and learn everything I could about what to expect. My friends were growing sick of me talking about it. Soon, however, they wouldn't have to worry, as the day of my departure was rapidly approaching, and I was already thinking of the new friends I'd be making in Orlando, all of whom would no doubt want to talk as much as I did about this grand adventure.

CHAPTER THREE

Arrival

May 5, 2012. In just 24 hours my flight would leave England. I had already pre-booked my seat and checked in on-line. Unfortunately, I wouldn't be able to sit next to the three other girls also bound for Disney who were on the same flight as me. One of them also attended University of Chester (not my superior interview partner, however!) and the other two went to college elsewhere, though they had come to Chester briefly for a day trip. I managed to get a seat on the same row as them, but we were separated by the aisle. Nevertheless, I was happy with this seating arrangement, because it meant I'd be close enough to them so that I could participate in the inevitable (and probably never-ending) Disney conversations as we crossed the Atlantic, but I'd also be able to relax and maybe even get in a nap. The four of us had been texting all evening before the flight, even as I tried to spend time with my mum before heading to bed early so I'd be awake and alert for the 5am flight. My dreams were of pixie dust, castles, and Mickey (no Russell, fortunately). The excitement was unbearable. I just wanted to be there already.

I had said goodbye to my brother the day before, and it was now time to say goodbye to my mum. I was a little bit sad, but mainly because I wanted to take them with me so they could enjoy America, too. I put my backpack down in the car and ran back to my mum for a second massive hug. It had to be massive, because it needed to last for three months, the duration of my program. I waved to her as I drove off.

Once on the road, I plugged in my iPod and listened to my generic Disney playlist, which meant only one thing when I had woken up a bit, and that a duet with my dad of "Under the Sea" as we drove two hours to Manchester airport. My dad unloaded my two suitcases from the car and stayed with me until the other girls arrived. We mingled for a while, as the parents discussed their Disney-crazed daughters and we laughed and squealed in excitement. When we heard the boarding announcement, there were tears all around, or almost all around, because I surprised myself by remaining composed and dry-eyed. I'm sure I looked heartless, but I knew that I'd be feeling much worse homesickness soon, and it wouldn't do my dad any good to see me in tears right before he left me at the airport. Finally, we broke away from our parents and took the escalators upstairs, in complete silence broken only by a few final sobs.

After jumping through all the hoops of airport security, we made it to our flight gate where we waited until our seat numbers were called and got in line. There were plenty of adults, but all with children. Some couples gave us funny looks for our giggly Disney conversation, my loud voice, and the general excitement bubble that had formed around us.

As we took our seats ready for the long 9-hour flight, we sucked on our sweets and prepared for takeoff. Contrary to what I had expected, there was very little Disney conversation, or any kind of conversation; most of the flight consisted of awkward silences (we were still comparative strangers, even though we had a common purpose), watching movies, and listening to music with only one earphone so we wouldn't look completely rude to the others. Before we knew it, we were putting our seatbelts back on and the plane was landing in Orlando.

Our dreams were about to become a reality. Once we got through Customs...

Unlike everyone else on our flight, we were the targets for loads of questions by the customs agents. They wanted to make sure we were going to leave when we were supposed to, that we had no plans to work illegally, and so forth. I didn't know much about customs; I'd only ever passed through with my parents, and they had never bothered us when we had been on holiday. This was an entirely different experience. The customs agents engaged us in what I thought was friendly conversation, but the did so to lull us into a false sense of security, making it easier for them to catch us in a lie. This happened to me. An agent asked me where I had come from and what I was studying back home. Then he asked me:

> Customs Guy: Where are you going to be working?
>
> Me: Disneyland.
>
> Customs Guy: You're in the wrong state for that.

This led to him asking me more questions, even after I stated that I had meant Disney World, not Disneyland. I had never gotten my parks confused before, and it was a sign of my excitement and nervousness that I had done so now.

After my Disneyland ordeal was over, and the customs guy decided I wasn't dangerous, we went to claim our luggage and find transportation. Our housing complex, Vista Way, was 20-30 minutes from the airport, which gave us plenty of time to take lots of photos. We had all moved on from the awkward stage, and now we were interacting as if we'd known each other for years. I proved it when I turned to Amy, one of the girls, and shouted *"READY?!"* in her face before taking a photo of the two of us. Little did I know that Amy would soon become one of my best friends and my rock during the program.

When we arrived at Vista Way, we were taken to a room where we sat through a welcome session which consisted of free cookies, chocolate, and bottled water. This is where I made even more of a fool of myself than I did by shouting "ready" in Amy's face. We got our apartment keys in a little sealed brown envelope. In the top corner was a label with our name and some numbers. Everyone was discussing what apartment they were in. Amy and Shauna were assigned to the same unit. I just stood, confused, looking at my paperwork and trying to see where everyone else was finding their apartment numbers. The only numbers I could were 2012. If I'd been asked where I was staying, all I would have been able to say was "Vista Way" and the current year. Amy giggled and came to my rescue: "Ema, that's not the year, you are in apartment number twenty twelve."

Even though I felt stupid, I forgot all about it when I realized that I'd be in the same apartment block as Amy and Shauna.

We headed over to our apartments to unpack a few essentials before heading over to one of the local Walmarts for the dreaded food shop. After carrying my suitcases up two flights of stairs, I entered 2012 and closed the door behind me. I saw a room directly to my left with nothing and no one in it, and so there's where I dropped my suitcases. The other bedroom was already occupied, though only by suitcases; no one was in there, and for now I had the apartment entirely to myself. I left in a few minutes for Walmart, hoping that when I got back I'd have a roommate.

The four of us from the Manchester flight regrouped and took public transportation to Walmart. Luckily, we had all brought our bedding with us, so we only had to worry about getting food. However, for the British, doing a food shop in an American supermarket was going to be difficult. Walmart was about four times the size of my Asda back home, if not bigger. I was tired, had endured a 9-hour flight, and the last thing I wanted to do was shop for enough food to last me two weeks. It wasn't as if we could skip any aisles, because we'd have no idea what we would miss. This trip led to multiple distractions, in particular the craft aisle for me, with its multitudes of scrapbooking paper and stickers. I'd be lucky if I found colored biros and a pack of highlighters at my supermarket back home. As much as I don't want to admit it, at least a third of the $90 I spent at Walmart was on items that I thought were cool.

After we went through the tills, we all congregated in the corner to re-bag, tactically putting bottles and heavy items in our backpacks. At this point, I was totally regretting my need to buy a 12-can pack of Diet Coke.

Once I had conquered getting onto the bus with a backpack that seemed heavier than the bus, I found a seat and stupidly put my frozen food bag on my lap. If the arctic air conditioning on the bus didn't freeze me, the food on my lap certainly would. Making matters worse, it seemed that every voice I heard on the bus spoke with a British accent. We all had to deal with the 22-kilogram weight restriction on the plane, and so we had to be selective with what we brought from home. As a result, we had to buy lots more stuff locally than the average American college program participant, who'd be able to stuff their car with everything imaginable if they were within driving distance of Disney World. The bus was well and truly packed with people and goods, leaving us little room to rearrange our purchases and forcing me to keep my little piece of the Arctic nestled on my lap.

We got back to Vista, finally, with some life still in my legs, and I soon learned that getting on the bus with my deadweight backpack was nowhere near as difficult as walking up the stairs to 2012 on the top floor. Making matters worse, it was dark, around 9:30pm, and my keys had gotten stuck on a cotton thread in my pocket, beneath the Walmart bags that were cutting off the circulation to my arms. I finally made it into the apartment where another surprise awaited me: the door to my room was closed. I was sure I'd left it open when I went out. Walking past it, I went straight to the kitchen to put away my frozen goods before they thawed completely. With that done, I went back to my room and opened the door. Inside I found a girl, a bit shorter than me, with hair as red as Ariel's. I was so excited to meet my summer roommate. She said:

"Hi, I'm Abbie"

CHAPTER FOUR

Orientation, Day One

The first thing on the agenda for my first full day in Florida was to pick up my housing ID. This all-important item would get me through the security gates at the housing complexes, onto the College Program buses, and as a photo ID to take advantage of Cast Member discounts in the parks.

My ID photo would be permanent for the entire program, so before I left the apartment I made sure to put on my makeup perfectly, hide my flaws with concealer, and pile on the eyeliner. When I got down to the pavilion to have my photo taken, I could feel the heat on my face. Thick makeup and Florida weather are not the perfect combination; however, what was about to happen was more embarrassing than the sweat running down my face and the smudged eyeliner. I got to the front of line and sat down on the chair, and the guy with the camera told me to do a "Disney Smile". I gave my biggest-ever smile and FLASH! The picture was taken. Now I had the goofiest ever smile on my ID, and people would be looking at it for the next three months. Great.

After getting our IDs, we all did a sharing session and looked at one another's photos, giggling at their silliness (real or imagined). Then we headed to The Commons, one of the other housing complexes, for a presentation about our housing complex. I sat next to Amy and we kept each other smiling with whispered non-Disney answers to Disney questions, like this one:

> Presentation woman: In Disney, what do you always wear?
>
> Me: Sunscreen.
>
> Amy: Underwear.
>
> Random Girl: A smile.
>
> Presentation Woman: Correct. A smile.

The presentation went on for about two hours and consisted mostly of boring but necessary rules and regulations. They told us about the importance of our IDs, having respect for our apartment mates (especially if you work a late shift and come home in the middle of the night), and so forth. This presentation was intended only for internationals, so they spent a lot of time going over immigration rules and visa restrictions. The main thing was what happens if we defy the rules, or if our visa becomes invalid because of the actions that we take; answer: we're put on the next flight home. In that circumstance, we also wouldn't get our 30 days of traveling time after the end of the program. If we were terminated, or if we decided to leave the program ourselves, we'd lose our visa immediately. There were a lot of things that could get us terminated, including underage drinking (in England, the legal age for drinking is 18, unlike in America, where it's 21, so that took some getting used to), sneaking into another housing complex, threatening a cast member, owning a weapon (even a toy weapon bought in the parks), and engaging in any illegal activity. To name a few.

After the presentation finished, we went back to our apartment to get ready for Starlight Splash, the College Program welcome party that night at Typhoon Lagoon. Attending the party would get us a free t-shirt, food, and access to all the rides. On top of that, there was a DJ and some pirates who came to dance to Nikki Minaj with us.

It started to rain while we were stood in line eating our Mickey ice cream sandwiches. I just picked the biscuit off mine because I don't like ice cream, but I couldn't say no to free food. However, rain and biscuit don't mix well, just like Florida heat and lots of makeup. We were already wet from being in the wave pool and the lazy river, so the rain wasn't bothering us too much, but it was definitely affecting my ice cream sandwich, and I let this be known to the group: "My soggy fingers are making my biscuit soggy."

This showed everyone my tendency to be a drama queen, but they couldn't help but laugh at my ridiculous statement.

CHAPTER FIVE

Orientation, Day Two

It was our second full day in Florida, and we still hadn't been to any of the parks except for Typhoon Lagoon the night before. I felt like a kid on the run-up week to Christmas as we waited outside at The Commons for the second orientation meeting to begin.

Cast members spoke to everyone, in groups of 6–8, before letting us inside. This was more like a personal inspection. They look at piercings, tattoos, and discussed any issues we had about Traditions, which was taking place the following day. The inspection wasn't to find flaws so they could send you home, but more of a reminder for you to cover up any tattoos and remove piercings, because if you turned up at Traditions with them, you would be sent away and told to attend another Traditions class later in the week. However, you aren't given your Disney ID card until you complete a Traditions class, and without your ID card, you can't work or play in the parks. On top of all that, they inspected our hair to ensure that it was in accord with the "Disney Look", and if it wasn't, we had less than 24 hours to correct the problem, either with a cut or dye. Unfortunately for Shauna, the cast members thought she might not make it into Traditions because she had the slightest hint of dip dye in her hair from years ago. It was only one or two shades lighter than her natural hair, and you could barely even see it. But there was no appeal to the strict Disney rules, and so rather than risk being barred from Traditions, Shauna got ride of that old dye.

I'd done a fair bit of reading prior to going on the program, and former ICPs had said that during the second orientation meeting we'd learn our job locations. This was what everyone was talking about. When we finally went into the presentation room, we were ushered to our aisle, as the paperwork was in alphabetical order. I wouldn't be able to sit next to my friends here. I saw my name on a piece of paperwork and sat down next to a Canadian guy who was chatting up the three girls in the row in front, and the girls were obviously fed up with him and immediately started talking to me. They were Canadian, too. Not long after I sat down, a Chinese lad took up the chair on the other side of me. I hoped he wasn't a creep, too. He started to read his paperwork, then he said:

"Where is the Grand Floridian?"

I was dying inside at the thought of someone not knowing their general Disney knowledge before they arrived. As these girls had started to speaking to me from the moment I sat down, and my attention was focused on making sure I didn't get into conversation with this creepy guy, I completely forgot about my work location. The moment the Chinese lad asked me where his resort was, I shot straight to my paperwork. I skimmed through all of it until I found the page that said "work location".

PORT ORLEANS!

I had never stayed or even visited Port Orleans before, but I had researched all the resorts before I came so I was pretty excited, because I remember it was themed on Mardi Gras and *Princess and the Frog*, and looked family friendly and fun.

The attention quickly flipped back to the Canadian Sir Creeps-a-Lot when he turned the conversation around back to himself. He started telling everyone around him, no matter how uninterested they were, that his suitcase had been lost on his flight to Orlando, and I felt a bit of sympathy for him and his fear that he wouldn't have anything to wear to Traditions the following day. However, I still didn't want to talk to him.

The presentation started, finally, with a review of the basic rules and community codes that we were taught yesterday. Then the immigration lady came to speak to us again, just in case we didn't already understand that drinking and owning a weapon was prohibited; this time, the point was pressed upon us with help from *Toy Story* and *Stitch* images, so we'd never forget. After we were scared stiff again by the thought that the slightest action could result in us being terminated and sent back home, we had to then fill out a long form to apply for a Social Security number. Luckily for us, the presenter talked us through the entire form, step by step.

After filling in all the paperwork, watching all the safety videos and testimonials from CP alumni, and absorbing every last ounce of information I could, I was even more excited about my upcoming

Traditions class the next day. I also felt nervous, which made my stomach feel like a shaken-up can of pop. Time to calm my nerves with a visit to Walgreens, located conveniently across the road from Vista Way. We all wanted to see what it had for sale, in the hope that we wouldn't have to trek to Walmart every time we needed minor items and supplies. Shauna also needed to pick out the right color hair dye, and she wanted to get that ordeal over with and her hair in proper order before we headed over to Downtown Disney for tea.

Back at Amy and Shauna's apartment, I agreed that I would dye Shauna's hair for her. It was only when I was half-way through that I realized we had known each other less that 72 hours and she had trusted me with picking the right shade dye and applying it to her hair. Safe to say, I was petrified that her hair would come out completely the wrong shade or go green. Lucky for me, well, mostly Shauna, it was a perfect match, and we were able to leave for our adventure at Downtown Disney in high spirits, ready to eat a stupid amount of food and try on silly hats.

CHAPTER SIX

Traditions

This is possibly one of the most important days in my life: Traditions. There were special buses available to take us to the morning class of Traditions on time, which in our case meant leaving Vista Way at 6:50am to arrive at Disney University by 8am. We were given strict instructions to make sure we there were on time. If we weren't, we'd have to be scheduled into another one, which would put us in a limbo for as long as a week.

Fortunately, I was scheduled for the same morning class as my roommate, which meant we wouldn't have to creep around to avoid waking the other person up. I walked down to the bus with Abbie in plenty of time, and we grabbed two seats together. We sat there for a while in silence, purely because we were both tired. I closed my eyes a few times in hopes of getting an extra 5 minutes of sleep on the bus, but my brain was too excited, even though my body disagreed.

It was 6:52. The bus hadn't left. I said to Abbie, "I thought the bus was leaving dead on 10 to 7; why haven't we left yet". Finally, the bus doors closed, but just as it was pulling away, a guy came running up and banged on the door. The driver was nice and let him on. The guy was wearing dark jeans and a shirt. He looked a mess, and far too informal for a Traditions class. He was heading to the back when he saw a spare seat behind us. I was still half asleep at this point, but it was only as he sat down that I realized it was Creepy Mike, the Canadian chatterbox from orientation the day before. I pretended not to see him and whispered to Abbie, who I'd already told about him, that it was *him*. We pretended to be asleep the whole journey to avoid communicating with Mike, but to be honest, it was 7 o clock in the morning, and I wasn't really pretending most of the time.

The bus pulled up at Disney University on schedule. I had seen pictures of this place online and had always thought that its sign had been Photoshopped. I didn't know such a place existed, and why

I couldn't go there to study. We headed inside to around all the people who had stopped outside to get their picture in front of the university sign. We decided to get ours later, when we'd look more alive.

Inside the building, we sat in the entrance area and glanced at the Disney cartoon playing on a TV behind us. There were Disney models on display, Disney paintings hung, and Disney quotes written on the walls. I absorbed every detail. I particularly liked Chip 'n' Dale floating down on parachutes from a missing ceiling tile gap. Before I had time to look at everything, we were split into our groups. Abbie was taken away from me at this point, but luckily I had Shauna with me, and a Canadian girl, Paige, who shared an apartment with Shauna. As we followed our leader up to our classroom, I tried to look at every wall, because each time you turned there was a new picture to see and story to read. One corridor had pictures and some writing dedicated to Disney animation artists. I love facts and trivia, and I really just want to stop and read them all. This building was practically a Disney Company Museum.

We stopped around the corner from the Disney Animators' hall of fame in a waiting area where one wall had Disney heroes on it and the opposite wall Disney villains. The montage of pictures was amazing. Best waiting area ever!

As the line started to move, I stopped focusing my attention on the walls and looked forward to see a table full on shiny blue cards. Our IDs! This was the holy grail of cards. Having one meant we were officially Disney cast members, it meant we were awesome, it meant we could go to the parks for free, it meant we had proof that we have the coolest job in the world, it meant we got discounts on Disney food and merchandise, it meant we were the coolest of all the cats.

After getting out IDs we headed into a room, which had even better walls than those outside in the corridors. We wanted a table with three spare seats so we could sit together, and we had to act quickly to find one. More people were coming in behind us and taking up the space. Finally, I spotted it, a table right at the front, and we grabbed it ahead of others with the same intention. In front of each seat was a baby blue workbook with a red stripe down the side, dotted with white Mickey heads. In the top right-hand corner was a empty name tag-shaped image. Then, in the middle, an even lighter blue watermarked "D", in the Disney font, and "Traditions, brought to you by Disney University" in black. Of course, looking at the front cover just wasn't enough, I had to have a cheeky look inside, but nothing gave away what we were going to be doing.

Disney knows that a lot of the essential information we had to know is a tad boring, and that's why they hire to most energetic, fun, and lively cast members for the Traditions team. Since this was my first program, I was completely immersed in the Disney Magic, to the point that even the thought of safety training seemed exciting.

The computer program started to teach us about how "SAFE D BEGINS WITH ME!" but at 8 o clock in the morning, this was harder than I had anticipated, even with Disney Magic spurring me on. I had to use all my will power to keep my eyelids from closing. I felt so guilty because I didn't want to seem rude or ungrateful to the cast members leading the class. Even animated clips of the famous "Chris, from Orlando" talking about the four keys of working for Disney didn't wake me up.

We moved on to filling out sections of the workbook. Actually doing something woke me up, and it helped that each activity was different. The first activity was to practice our Disney point, and learning our Disney point was lesson number one of why Disney has such great customer service. They think of everything, down to the last detail. They tell you that the Disney point was created because in some cultures pointing with one finger is considered rude, but most importantly small children could associate pointing with one finger with being in trouble, as a parent may "wag" one finger at them when telling their child off. Therefore, Disney created their own point, which is unique to the Disney Company, so if a guest were to ask you about the closest place to purchase ice cream, instead of using your index finger to show them the way, you would direct them there by pointing with your index and middle finger together, or alternatively you can direct with your whole hand. To be able to practice, we needed something to point at, and as part of this exercise we were told each table had to pick a team leader. On the count of three, we were told to point at the person we thought would make the best team leader.

One...I knew I didn't know anyone that well...

Two...I think Paige would make a good leader...

Three.....I point at Paige.

But four (technically eight, with the Disney Point rules) fingers are pointed at me. The best part of this was that it won me a 'critter', a little plastic toy of one of the Fab 5 (Mickey, Minnie, Donald, Goofy, and Pluto) that are given out as prizes during the class.

We engaged in multiple mini-competitions throughout the morning, most of which involved us answering questions about Walt Disney, his characters, the parks, and the company as a whole. Each correct answer won you a critter. We spent the rest of our morning watching videos starring current and past cast members talking about their experiences. People shared their "magic moments" from their trips to the parks as guests. Finally, right before our scheduled break time, we watched a montage video made up of cartoon clips from various films, interspersed with past and present cast members talking about the company. Most of us had become a bit emotional at this point, and this probably had something to do with the heart-grabbing music playing behind the video clips. Everyone in the room clearly shared the same ambition of working for Disney, and therefore, in this moment, everyone realized their dream was coming true when a clip of Walt Disney himself welcomed us to the family. Obviously, he didn't rise from the dead; he had filmed a welcome message for everyone who was to ever work for his company, and he had done so to personally welcome them to his family, even after he was gone, and to thank them for being a part of his dream and keeping his spirit alive.

After I had composed myself and wiped away my tears, I went with Shauna during our break to Company D, a cast member-only store located inside the university that sold limited edition merchandise, such as hoodies and tote bags, but the best thing was the pins. I bought myself two pins and a lanyard for my ID.

When we returned from our break, the class was split into two teams, since taking the entire class as a single unit for the backstage walking tour of the Magic Kingdom would have been unwieldy. I was glad that I'd chosen to wear flat, comfortable shoes, unlike some of the Barbies in their 8" heels. We picked up headsets as we left the room en route to the Magic Kingdom, a warning fresh in our heads that no photos or videos of backstage areas was allowed, with immediate termination the fate of those who disobeyed.

After we took our tour through the Utilidors (tunnels), we head through some doors, and some more doors, and then up some stairs and though another door, and as if by magic we were on a side street of Main Street, U.S.A.! I could smell the sweet pastries from the ice cream parlor.

We walked down Main Street as our leaders pointed out multiple cast members who were giving good customer service. Every cast member we saw had once been in our place, and they knew who we were, walking in our tight little groups with headsets firmly in place. They were sure to say, "Hello, Traditions People", and welcomed us into the Disney family.

Back in the classroom, I was never so glad for air conditioning. As we settled back into our seat and turned in our headsets, there was a knock at the door. Who should it be other than the boss himself, Mickey Mouse. Not only did he come to say "hi", he brought him with some important items: our nametags! Mickey stood at the front, and table by table we got into an orderly line to collect our nametags and then sit back down, where we took photos of our nametags, my nametag with the critter next to it, us wearing our nametags, us wearing our nametags in a group...you get the idea, there were a lot of pictures taken of nametags.

Finally, we said goodbye to Mickey, watched one last inspirational video from Walt, and then we were sent into the big wide world as official Disney cast members.

CHAPTER SEVEN

My First Trip as a Cast Member

First point of call, Guest Relations. We had just embarked on a huge journey, and we wanted to let everyone know that we were new cast members, and what's the best way to let everyone know you are celebrating something special than with a celebration button! We picked up our "My First Trip" buttons and asked for the Guest Relations cast member to write "as a cast member" underneath. Automatically, her first words weren't "yes" but "Congratulations". Every cast member we saw that day congratulated us and welcomed us to the Disney family with the most genuine of smiles.

We headed straight for Space Mountain, and got in the 30-minute line, which actually was a minimal line of 10 minutes. We split into teams of 3 and jetted off into outer space at the speed of light.

After going on a few other rides, we hung around Main Street waiting for the Move It, Shake It parade to begin. We danced with the characters and the stilt walkers. This was such a fun way to start our program. It really felt like I was on holiday.

With 9 of us in the group, it was hard to agree on what to do next. The heat had become unbearable. Some of us wanted to go back on Space Mountain and other rides, but Amy, Shauna, and myself, who were suffering most from the heat, decided to go make use of our Disney IDs and get discount on merchandise. We had already picked out a few things that we wanted when we saw it in Downtown Disney, but had refrained from buying it since we knew we'd be able to pay less in a day or two. I wanted pins. I'd been on holiday to Disney World before, and my brother had bought loads of pins and started trading with the cast members, who kindly gave him a crash course on how trading worked. I wasn't as much into pin trading as I was pin collecting. However, I saw how much fun my brother had had, and so decided to add "start pin trading" to my bucket list for the summer. We went to the Emporium where I bought a Mr Pricklepants pin, after the team name of my Traditions class, and two other pins: the grape soda bottle top badge from *Up* and Sorcerer Mickey (because it reminds me of Fantasmic!, my favorite thing to do on Disney property).

As we were leaving the Magic Kingdom for our air-conditioned apartments, there was a little girl, maybe 4 or 5 years old, just entering the park holding hands with her mum. I could see the wonder and magic in her eyes; she was taken aback by the beauty of the Magic Kingdom. Then she said, in a mesmerized voice;

"Mummy, is this a dream?"

This girl's response to the magic showed me how much every child and adult enjoys being in Disney and how much I'm going to love contributing to making that magic happen for every family that I see.

CHAPTER EIGHT

Role Orientation

"Oh, you mean chips. You British people make my day with your funny words."

This was the response I got for my stupidity of asking, "Where can I find the crisps?"

Although the initial look I received in response to this question was hysterical, the assistant at Walgreens had no idea what I was on about. I was glad I could make her laugh at my expense; I enjoy making people laugh, but I really just wanted some Pringles.

Today was May 10. I'd been in Florida for 5 days, and I wasn't used to saying the correct word for what I wanted—I kept asking for chips and getting a packet of crisps. I definitely wasn't used to the backwards dates, or being 5 hours behind.

For my fifth day in Florida, I was going to have my first encounter with what I would spend my summer doing. I traveled to Disney University once again for a class called Housekeeping Core. I can't say the title of the class overly excited me. One of the girls who was on my flight, Charlie, was going to be a housekeeper at the Polynesian, so she was taking the class, too. It was another early morning, and we'd been watching multiple videos on various topics that were supposed to be useful to us, like blood-borne pathogens. I wasn't feeling the magic. I was bored out of my brain and hadn't come here to watch videos of bloody bedsheets. I probably would have learned a lot more had I been passionate about what my role involved. But really, who can be that passionate about cleaning up after someone? I did perk up every time there was a video from a cast member talking about their experiences of guest interaction.

Next, we went to a computer room where we completed a number of online assessments. These covered all the topics that we had been taught throughout the morning. I panicked. I knew I should have paid more attention. *I'm totally going to fail this, and then they'll send me home!* Each assessment was more daunting than the next, and I was very much aware that I had to pass the them all to progress to the next stage, on-the-job training.

And what do you know: I passed. I don't think Disney wants anyone to fail, not at this point.

After the assessments and a short, much-needed break, the class leaders shared some Housekeeping stories, which became more of an informal chat and a welcome respite from the boring stuff. We heard some of their personal stories, and even a few legendary ones. They introduced the stories by telling the basic rules about entering a room and finding an unattended child or unauthorized pets or animals. One story, in particular, stayed with me:

One of the class leaders was working on the front desk in a Disney resort at the time of the incident. The housekeeper had encountered something very rare. She knocked on the door and, having gotten no response from any guests inside the room, opened it to reveal a cow standing between the beds and the TV. If you think that's funny, then it gets better: this room was on the second floor, and whoever put the cow there had to get it onto Disney property and past all the cast members working at the resort, before taking it to the second floor.

The moral of the story: EXPECT EVERYTHING.

CHAPTER NINE

Location Training

The second day of training was my location orientation at Port Orleans Cast Services. My roommate Abbie was also working at Port Orleans in Quick Service, which meant we had the same location training and could get the bus together.

Our class was due to start at 8:30am. We were going to be getting bus D. The college program buses are lettered, and each bus goes to various resorts, parks, and recreational locations off Disney property. It was going to be the first time either of us had got on bus D, and it would soon become our second home as we would use it every day to get to and from work. Cast Services is the hub for the cast members working at the resort, with lockers and wardrobe for our costumes, and where we could drop off old costumes to be washed and pick up fresh ones. Port Orleans is actually two resorts—Riverside and French Quarter—and the bus stops at each, plus the central Cast Services, and we had to remember to get off at the right stop.

We arrived at Cast Services (known here as "Jazz Alley") to find a lot of people rushing around, but we ignored them and followed the signs to a room off the main corridor where we found a few people sitting at tables. All of these people were middle-aged, and I felt very young walking in on them. As Abbie and I sat down at our own table, a male Disney cast member came over to us and introduced himself as our trainer for the day. He gave us some plastic colorful, metallic, Mardi Gras necklaces. That, and the glitter all over the table, made me feel like I'd stepped into a kid's school disco. But there was also free cookies and pop, and I did judge myself a bit for eating three cookies and drinking a can of Diet Coke at 8:15 in the morning, all on an empty stomach.

After everyone arrived, I realized that the two of us were the youngest in the room, and the only non-Americans, and the only ones who were on the college program. Obviously, the first activity we were going to do had to be a "let's get to know each other" task. It required us to pick a colored coin out of a hat. The color of the coin corresponded to an additional question we had to answer on top of the basic set of name, where are you from, and what role do you have. My additional question was to name my favorite Disney character.

Port Orleans French Quarter is themed on New Orleans and Mardi Gras, and its sister resort, Riverside, on the antebellum South. Riverside then splits again into Magnolia, which has the royal Princess rooms, and Alligator Bayou, which is themed on *Princess and the Frog*. We had a PowerPoint presentation where we learned basic information on the whole resort, such as when it opened and how many rooms are available.

We then went on a tour of both Riverside and French Quarter, taking us from the front desk and the grounds to children's activities. When we got back to Cast Services, the Housekeeping manager was there to greet the new cast members and to see if whether he had any newbies joining his group. He seemed excited when he realized I was joining, and even more so when he heard me speak and found out I was British. He looked just like the man from the Skittles advert (well, at least the one we have in our Skittles adverts).

I still wasn't overly excited, even after seeing the resort and hearing Housekeeping stories, but I was keen to get my costume and move on to the on-the-job training. I just kept telling myself it was a huge opportunity and that loads of people who didn't make it to the second interview would kill to be in my position.

Positive thinking was going to key here!

It got a bit better when the Costuming Department measured us and picked out a set of sizes to try on and see what we were most comfortable in. We could always change our sizes whenever we returned our old costumes. You can have four sets of your full costumes out at any one time. My full set consisted of a skirt, apron, and shirt. The system doesn't work so well for everyone, because some of us don't have access to Costuming everyday—for example, Abbie gets off the bus at French Quarter, not at Cast Services, which is the next stop. Even though it was a pain to have to wait for a bus from French Quarter to Cast Services, and then have to wait for an hour for a bus from Cast Services back to the apartment, she had it easier than most. I knew of some cast members whose Cast Services was a stop before their resort, which meant they either had to get up earlier and go there before work (as long as they weren't at work earlier than Costuming opened!) or spend part of their day off getting fresh costumes. But I also knew people who just washed their own costumes because it was too much hassle to take them back. It isn't mandatory for you to have Disney wash your costumes.

After collecting our costumes, I spent about 20 minutes laughing with Abbie over the fact that she is the girl with hair redder than Ariel's, and she gets the orangutan orange costume!

With that out of our systems, we returned to Jazz Alley where we were given more fizzy drinks and chocolate before we were sent into the big wide world ready to start on the job training.

CHAPTER TEN

On-the-Job Training

There is only so much that you can learn from watching PowerPoints and videos and listening to stories. After having two days of doing just that, it was time for me to learn the job I'd be doing for the next three months. I still hadn't had a day off to go enjoy myself in the theme parks, and I especially wanted to visit Hollywood Studios. But first I had four full days of training to get through. I was to start work at 8am, which meant I had to board the bus just before 7, but to save myself the stress of cutting it so closely, I decided to take the earlier 6:30 bus instead. We were told during orientation, and I'd read the same on many blogs, to never expect that a bus will get you to work on time. They were not kidding.

On the bus that first morning, there were a few people wearing the same costume as me, but I didn't dare talk to them as they all had earphones in, and I didn't feel that I had gained the right to talk to them first. It felt like a high school hierarchy; they were the jocks and I was the geek in the library who sat on their own at lunch. Once I got to Cast Services, I had a 45-minute wait, but luckily there was a TV in the canteen and this began my love for American television shows.

I saw plenty of women sitting in the canteen, and the only way I could tell that they were in Housekeeping was because they are wearing the same costume as I was wearing. The Disney magic seemed to stop at the door here; I got my share of dirty looks as I walked around the canteen looking for a place to sit. I was hoping that someone would swoop over and take me under their wing. This never happened, and between the dirty looks and the foreign language most of the other women were speaking, I quickly got the impression that I was not welcome here.

I didn't speak to anyone all day that wasn't a trainer or a manager, despite my efforts to be polite and smile at everyone, without having it reciprocated. I soon learned that the full-time cast members don't like internationals because they think we are here to take jobs from them, and the part-timers don't like college program cast members in general because it is hard enough for them fighting to get full-time status or extra hours without us taking the hours.

As I was given no direction as to where to go once I arrived at Casting, I just followed a group of people dressed the same as me. I found myself faced with an overwhelming number of people who didn't speak English as their first language. I wandered over to a huge room with two blocks of chairs set out like an assembly hall at school. After being told I couldn't have a particular chair because it was being saved for someone else—twice!—I finally found somewhere to sit.

Once the manager came and it looked like everyone was here, I noticed that one of the chairs where I had asked to sit in was empty. I felt sick at the thought of someone lying to me just because they didn't want to sit next to the new British girl. I was looking around in hopes that someone knew who I was, and that they would show me where to go. Only by chance did I see a green folder on a lady's lap with my name on it. I made a beeline for her. Even though her name tag said "Jenny", I could tell English wasn't her first language because she looked confused when I said "excuse me." I pointed at the name on the folder and said "that's me." She laughed and said "I understand." I think she found it funny, because she could tell that I knew English wasn't her first language, but saying "that's me" was maybe a bit too basic, and probably sounded very funny to someone that did understand.

Jenny was from Puerto Rico, like a lot of the housekeepers at Port Orleans. Although she did, in fact, speak very good English, there were moments when I could tell she didn't understand me, but with my accent and the speed at which I speak, I don't blame her. I spent the first two days with Jenny. She would show me what to do and how to perform each job.

The first thing we had to do was get a pargo. Pargos are like little golf carts that are used to get the housekeepers from Cast Services to their work locations at the resort. Before we could do that, however, I had to go get a "Royal' apron. It was blue and yellow and I didn't like it as much as my white one which made me look like Cinderella. So it was back to Costuming to find an apron in my size, scan my ID so it went on my costuming log, and then off to find a pargo going to our assigned section of the resort. Once we got on the pargo and traveled to Riverside, we went straight to a linen room. These were behind doors that looked like every other door, but had a plate on them that read "Cast Members Only".

It was quite exciting to have access to cast member-only room, even if it was just full of towels. As lovely as Jenny was, her co-workers weren't so welcoming and kept talking to her and to each other in Spanish, looking at me and talking to each other again. I felt so awkward not being able to join in with the conversation. What made it worse is I knew they could speak English, because they spoke to the manager in English.

It wasn't all negative that day. I found my first hidden Mickey in the design printed on a table in one of the guest rooms. Jenny was really excited to point the hidden Mickeys out to me. I also got my first tip of $2. Technically, it was Jenny's, but she halved everything with me, which I thought was the nicest thing, because these women really do work hard and the extra money in tips means a lot, so for her to share it all with me was a kind gesture and very much appreciated.

I had the most fun learning how to make towel animals. Before I left for Disney, I'd seen a video of an elephant being made out of a towel. I really wanted to learn how to make it, and Jenny taught me on my first day.

On the second day, Jenny started giving me my own section of the room to clean and would then come over and assess how well I did and tell me where I needed to improve, because on my third day I'd have my own cart and my own board with my own rooms.

I knew nothing of carts or boards at this stage, but I quickly had to learn. The carts were the simplest things to work out; they had all the equipment and supplies we needed to clean. The boards were pretty easy to follow. They consisted of a piece of paper with a table on it, each row for a different room, and they were color-coded based on room status. White meant an occupied room with a guest who was going to be in that room again that night. Blue meant that a linen change was required, and pink meant that a family was checking out. There is more to do in a checkout room than in an occupied room, and so if you had a lot of pink on your board, you knew that it is going to be a rushed day to make sure you get all the rooms done in time.

On my last day shadowing Jenny, I was to sit for an exam-style, multiple-choice assessment as well as cleaning a whole room, as a checkout, on my own, which would also be assessed. I found the room cleaning part really easy. I kept a list of all the tasks I had to do to make sure I didn't miss anything. I passed both parts of the assessment, which meant that the next day I could be completely on my own.

The next six days of training were called 'ramp up'. This was a slow way to introduce a new cast member to Housekeeping. The first day I started with 8 rooms, then I got an additional 2 rooms added to my board on each subsequent day. On the sixth day I was scheduled to work only from 8:30am til 12:30pm, which let me get back to the apartment and chill.

Although I didn't feel like I was a housekeeper, or belonged in the Housekeeping community, I had passed my tests with flying colors, and Ema had earned her ears. I could now remove the tell-tale red training sash under my nametag.

CHAPTER ELEVEN

A Meeting with Mickey

I knew I had read about people switching roles if they'd had allergic reactions to the chemicals, and I was certain I'd read some stories about other college program participants who had transferred roles after being successful at an Entertainment audition.

There is an International Service Centre at Vista Way. The people there had spoken to us during our orientation meetings, and they were to be our Floridian "parents" during the program. I thought I'd take my chances and pay them a visit. I'd planned out what I would say and thought I could try and win my case to be transferred to a different role. Even thinking about expressing how much I didn't enjoy Housekeeping made me tear up, and telling myself "I'm not gonna cry" made it worse. I couldn't fault the service center for trying their best for me; they fed me cookies, coke, and chocolate, as they could see I was very upset. However, what I wanted was out of their hands. I filled out a form which briefly explained my issue, complete with a tear-drop stain from the one I couldn't hold back that had rolled down my cheek and onto the paper before I could stop it.

I waited 5 minutes. In that time, a fresh batch of cookies had come out the oven, and I was the chosen tester for the batch (warm cookies are my favorite, especially when the dough is gooey and the chocolate still melted). Then they told me I could go and see Mickey. This confused me. I was emotional, and they were telling me I was going to talk to the mouse himself about my problem. Of course, it wasn't Mickey Mouse. This guy was even better; he was bubbly and full of life, and even when he was telling me the worst news, he still tried to keep me smiling. The general gist was that my visa restricted me from transferring and the stories I had read were probably all accounts from American participants (who therefore had no visa restrictions). Although this bad news meant no transfer, Mickey did try to help and contacted an Entertainment manager for me to "meet and greet" on my next day off. I was really disappointed that I couldn't transfer, but I was excited at the prospect of talking to someone doing a job in a department where was dying to work.

The moral of the story is: Do not tick or accept a role you aren't 100% sure you'll enjoy!

Mickey also told me to speak to my managers, because I might be able to get an internal transfer within my role which wouldn't jeopardize my visa. Since my visa application required me to list a specific role, I'd have to update it with any change in that role, and that would give the government an option to take away my visa, and my eligibility to remain in the U.S. for the college program. Despite Mickey's advice, I didn't want to chance it. And moreover, I didn't want to make the situation worse by letting my managers know that I was unhappy with my role. I didn't want to be seen as negative or ungrateful, and I didn't want to risk people thinking that any mistakes I made were not of the accidental variety but rather the result of me not caring about the job.

At this point, I'd been transferred from Magnolia to the main section of Port Orleans, and then transferred again to my permanent post at French Quarter. There was a lot more activity here, and the building where I usually worked was right next to the pool, so I could hear the music that was played during kid's activities.

As a CP, I didn't have the privilege of cleaning the same rooms every day. I was given the leftovers, or told to cover for other housekeepers on their days off. Being in a different part of the resort meant different managers, as well. In general, they tried their best to make me feel at home. I even confided to one of the managers, Jill, about my problems with the role. I had a bit of a clash with one of the other managers, since she was determined to get me into trouble for the smallest of infractions. Jill, fortunately, got the ball rolling to have me trained as a runner, where I would have more guest interaction, and hopefully a happier experience.

I had yet another training class, and this meant I got a short board. My class was at 2pm, so I finished my rooms by 12:30 and then had some lunch. I made a little nest in the linen room with a pile of towels and sat on the floor. After I'd finished my Lunchable, chocolate bar, and bottle of water, I went to stand by the stairs near the rooms I'd been given that day. Jason, one of the managers, showed up at 1:40, and said he had sent a runner to come get me, but they were a no-show. So he rang another runner and waited with me until she came. Her name was Hasnet. Such a unique name, I thought to myself. She was American, as well. I had no idea that there were people my age here at Port Orleans speaking English as their first language.

This was a turning point!

CHAPTER TWELVE

The Ronnie Who Wasn't

The next week of work was easier. On May 27, I finally felt like I was working at Disney. I was engaging in more guest interaction. One oblivious guest even asked me: *"Can you tell me how to get to Disney World?"*

As a cast member, you are trained to translate stupid questions like these. And what this guest actually meant by "Disney World" was "Magic Kingdom". After confirming that Magic Kingdom was her destination, to which she giggled upon realizing how silly she must have sounded, I directed her to the bus stop and wished her a magical day. In addition to the guest interaction, I had learned that I could also enjoy Housekeeping. I was getting on average $20–30 in tips per day. On top of that, I was able to help myself to a variety of groceries and snacks that guests left behind in check-out rooms.

The first part of the morning was like a primary school assembly. The room was freezing, so I started to bring a top with me to wear over my costume during the presentation. Little did I know at the time that this was going to be a topic of conversation amongst the managers. But this is a story you will get in full later. Even after being in my role for a month, waiting for the sheet of paper which had my board printed on it was a nerve-wracking process. Luckily, this day I had the same rooms as the day before and that meant:

- 1 linen change
- 5 check outs
- 11 occupied rooms

When I got to my building, I took the stairs to the floor where I'd be working. I always took the stairs, even though all of the other housekeepers head straight for the elevator. On this day, I passed by an overweight couple who gave me a look somewhere between disgust and confusion. I couldn't understand why: I was wearing a clean uniform, my face was as good as it was ever going to get, and I hadn't spoke so they couldn't tell that I wasn't American (in case they didn't like the British). Most of the housekeepers had looked at me in this exact same way when I walked into the canteen on my first day. Maybe they felt I made them look bad by taking the stairs when the elevator was right there (and which they took to their own floor).

I entered the linen room to get my cart and saw that I'd be sharing my floor with some very friendly Haitian women. Over half of the Port Orleans Housekeeping staff is Puerto Rican or Spanish-speaking, and the rest are mostly Haitians who speak Creole, a merged language of African and French. The Haitian were far more welcoming than the Spanish-speaking cast members. I had made friends with these two ladies. One took my board from me, and with my past experiences with the behavior of the housekeepers, I thought I might not be getting it back. She scribbled my numbers down on a piece of paper and handed me back my board. I was clueless. She tried to explain to me what she just did, and I politely smiled and nodded, but honestly, I had no idea what she had said. I didn't want to seem ungrateful that she was trying to be nice, and I appreciated them attempting to make conversation with me.

When it came to 12:30pm, I was getting hungry, but knew I needed to finish this room. Just moments later, the two Haitian ladies peered through my room's window and then knocked on the door. They had come to help me finish so I could come to lunch with them.

That's why she wanted my room numbers!

It was the nicest thing anyone had done for me to date. They also came to help me finish by 3:30pm so I could turn in my board on time. I hadn't worked for the company for 90 days, unlike my new friends, and so I couldn't clock out early. I spent the last few minutes of my shift sitting in the canteen with a holographic Tinker Bell balloon left behind in a check-out room by a guest, watching *Bolt* on ABC, and munching on brownies and Diet Coke (which had been left behind in one of my other rooms).

Later, as I sat in the canteen until it was time to go outside in the sun and queue up for the bus, a cast member named Ronnie walks in. We chatted for a bit while he waited for two of his friends. We all went to clock out together. I told him I was to the bus stop, and Ronnie said that he lived in Chatham and would be glad to drive me back to Vista. I don't really know how it happened, but as I went to get into his car, the top of my cheekbone bounced off the door frame. I quickly got into the car and pretended like nothing had happened. I chatted away the whole journey back and couldn't believe it had taken me a month to meet these people. I was acting totally normal, even though I wasn't able to blink and my eye socket felt like there was something that stopped my eye from closing the entire way when I tried to shut it. I could feel the swelling and knew that if I didn't get some ice on it soon, I was going to have a massive egg on the left side of my face. I recognize the road we were on and knew we were getting close to Vista. I was trying to inconspicuously catch a glimpse of my eye in the mirror to see whether there were any visible signs of what I had done. There was nothing to see. Just as we turned in by Walgreens to enter Vista, the heavens opened. It was normal in Florida to have a torrential downpour in the afternoon with no forewarning. Ronnie drove me to my apartment block to minimize the time I'd have to walk in the rain.

The next day was the cherry on top of a brilliantly turned-around week. Although I was ridiculously tired because I hadn't slept much due to the violent thunderstorms and the minor black eye from my face making friends with Ronnie's car, this day was like nothing I could have anticipated. I actually had friends and was enjoying myself. I had a "good" board with 5 linen changes and 12 occupied rooms. Ronnie was my "houseperson", and after doing a full round of the building he'd come help me with my rooms. He finished my 2 remaining linen changes with me, leaving me with only 4 occupied at 12:30pm.

Ronnie came back to get me when he was going for lunch. I had brought a bag of snacks with me, as it was easier to grab little things throughout the day just in case I got a bad board and wouldn't have time to stop and eat. Ronnie asked me if I fancied going out for lunch. He mentioned a few of his favorite places nearby, and when I said I'd never been to a restaurant called Steak 'n Shake, that decided it, because apparently I had to try it. So Ronnie drove us to Steak 'n Shake, where I was overwhelmed by the menu. I had a steak burger and fries, with a chocolate chip cookie dough milkshake from the special menu. There were so many shakes to choose from, and I did just want to try them all. The best part about it was that my lunch was technically free, because I'd paid for it with the tips that I had made that morning.

After having an amazing lunch, I returned to reality. As Ronnie and I were talking, he referred to someone calling him "Dan". I was confused, and I questioned that Dan was a weird nickname for Ronnie. But, as Ronnie explained, his real name was Dan, and he changed his nametag when people started calling him Ronnie. This was after he forgot his nametag one day. It is Disney policy that you must wear a nametag when you are working, which means that if you forget yours, Costuming will lend you a replacement. As a result, a lot of cast members become "Chris from Orlando" at some point in their Disney working lives. At other times, you might get a replacement nametag with a hometown that doesn't match your accent. Shauna, who worked at the Main Street Ice Cream Parlor, forgot her nametag one day, and got the famous Chris. She was stopped by multiple guests to tell her that she had a funny accent for an American; one guest going into great detail about how she managed to move from England to Orlando. But in Dan's case, he had been given a Ronnie nametag, not a Chris nametag, and the nickname caught on amongst his friends, leading him to request a permanent Ronnie.

CHAPTER THIRTEEN

Homesickness

No one prepares you for how bad homesickness feels. It was like a dull ache for the first month, and every time I thought about my family and home, I broke into tears. I convinced myself that it was because I didn't enjoy my job, and that I was just being emotional, not homesick

The program certainly wasn't what I had expected. I had high hopes for what I could achieve while at Disney, and I was getting nowhere. I never really thought about Housekeeping as a job; I was just excited to be living and working at Disney. I'd written a rather intense journal entry on June 17, and I'd never wish for anyone to see what I wrote because it isn't like me at all.

June 17, of course, is Father's Day, and as usual my alarm went off for work, but I was already awake because Abbie's alarm had gone off 30 minutes before mine. I didn't mind. I finally got out of bed and began to get ready. Abbie had rushed off to scoff down some breakfast, leaving me with the room to myself and 40 minutes before I needed to catch my bus. I had planned to ring home to wish my dad a happy father's day. After two failed attempts at adding the international code, it was third time lucky and hearing my dads voice was great. However, the second I hung up the phone, the sick feeling set in, and the tears streamed down my face.

Just as well I had half an hour to redo my makeup.

CHAPTER FOURTEEN

Abbie Bought a Blanket

June had come around so quickly, and it never slowed down. A new batch of college program participants were arriving this month. After telling them about my experiences, and making "enemies" for being at Disney a month before them, their dreams were about to become a reality.

I was especially excited about meeting a girl named Becca, who'd also been placed in Housekeeping. I had told her both the good and the bad. I wasn't going to lie to her and tell her that Housekeeping is the best job in the world. I had said it depends on the resort. As it turned out, she was assigned to Port Orleans, and I'd be taking her under my wing. I found this out while taking a re-evaluating progress assessment. Sitting in the office waiting for my results, I passed the time by looking at all the Disney fandangles on every shelf and ledge, and then I caught sight of a bunch of green training folders, one with Becca's name on it. I chose not to tell her, because finding out your location during orientation is exciting and I didn't want to spoil the surprise for her.

Along with the June arrivals, another special guests was arriving: my university lecturer Martin Metcalfe, who taught events management. This is the same lecturer I spoke about in chapter 1, when I went to University of Chester's open day. So this man has been a pretty influential part in my Disney journey. He knew the hardship I was going through. He convinced me to stay, and after I met with him, he went to speak to the international recruiter on my behalf to assist with application for the following year.

A couple of days later, we had a real-life Tower of Terror thunderstorm. The sky lit up, and the lightning was so scarily perfect that it could have been Photoshopped. The storm happened on June 10, when the second lot of English participants arrived. These storms continued through the night, leaving me no option but to call in sick the following day. It was also Abbie's day off. After having a lie in, Abbie made us both pancakes for breakfast. I couldn't go to the parks because I couldn't use my ID (penalty for calling in sick) so we decided to make a trip to Cast Connections, a discount store exclusively for cast members. Abbie was terrible (in a good way) at not spending her money. She didn't buy any Disney merchandise or much of anything not essential. She spent money on food. She didn't see bedding as essential, and as she chose not to bring any with her, she went a whole month just using her duvet cover and towels in a pillow case. Today, however, she finally bought a blanket, a children's blue Disney patterns blanket, with armholes. I had to talk her into buying it.

CHAPTER FIFTEEN

Runner Training

The day before I'd had a bit of a rough time. I had an issue with one of my managers who didn't seem to like me very much, even though she would tell me, quite frequently, how much she did—she certainly had a funny way of showing it.

On this day, she tried to get me in trouble for the second time since I had moved to her area at the French Quarter. It had to do with how I had cleaned a room, but it was how they'd trained me to do it, and none of the other housekeepers were getting into trouble for the nitty gritty bits which she said matter so much to the company. (Which they do; Disney prides itself on perfection. But enforcing that perfection should be consistent.) What bothered me was that she was singling me out, and it felt like I'd gone all the way back to square one, to my first day on the job, when I felt different and unwelcome. Fortunately, managers often change their locations, and soon another manager, Jill, who I liked very much, came to my section.

I went into Jill's office to chat. We discussed a lot of informal stuff, and then Jill asked what she could do to make my role more enjoyable for me. I mentioned to that I had been ready to self-term (leave the program voluntarily) and go back home when I learned that I wouldn't be able to transfer to a different role. She offered to help me get runner training as soon as possible. One of my friends, Trent, was a runner at Riverside, and I was always jealous of how much fun he seemed to have. A runner has their own radio, and guests and housekeepers can contact base to request items, whereupon base contacts the runner to deliver those items.

The following day, I came into work expecting the worst. Jill had promised, but I didn't want to get my hopes up. My luck, however, had changed! I was put right into my first day of runner training.

My trainer was a guy I had never seen before, an American named Johnny. We spent the entire day together as "Runner 1". Johnny explained how there were numerous runners at each resort because it would be virtually impossible for one person to handle all the requests. At French Quarter, there were three runners, and the resort was split into three areas:

- Runner 1: Buildings 1, 2, and the 3rd floor of building 3
- Runner 2: Buildings 4, 5, and the 2nd floor of building 3
- Runner 3: Buildings 6, 7, and the 1st floor of building 3

All the calls you got throughout the day were for requests within the same area, and although you were given a pargo, it made life too difficult to be darting back and forward across the entire resort for the smallest things. So it made sense to split up the duties between multiple runners and limit them to specific areas of the resort. Then, if a guest calls in for shampoo, he won't have to wait for the sole runner to finish his current job, source the shampoo, and drive it over.

I spent the whole day with Johnny doing Runner 1's job. We got a call sheet where we could write down all our requests because the radio could only hold a certain number of messages, and you had to have an additional way to keep track of your requests without having to faff around with technology. It was an insightful day. We got to deliver everything that a runner has to deliver, so I got to see where it all was kept. I did learn that this job literally lives up to its name, because you don't walk when trying to source the items, since you rarely find what you need in the first place where you look, and Disney gives you only a 15-minute window to fulfill guest requests. Johnny and I would wait for a call to come in, and then we would go on our adventures to source the required item. In between the calls, he spent a lot of time asking me questions about England whenever I didn't have any runner questions for him, and he also taught me how to drive the pargo, with him reminding me several times: *"We don't drive on the left here."*

CHAPTER SIXTEEN
ADO

It was safe to say this change to my role made all the difference to my program, because without it I could feel my enthusiasm slipping, and although I'm a pretty strong person, I felt myself very close to self-terming a number of times. Some days, after getting off the bus from work, I even came close to walking to the International Service Centre to tell them that I'd had it, without telling my friends first. But I'd always taken a deep breath and walked the long way to my apartment.

If you're in the program and think you have no choice but to self-term, don't. It will be the biggest regret of your life. There is so much that Disney can offer to help you through the bad times. I had the best support network, and although I chose not to tell my friends the one time I came closest to self-terming, I knew that they would be able to talk me out of it, which is why I didn't want to say anything. But the reason I walked away from the service center that day and back to my apartment was because I knew that whatever my friends would have to say, they would be right. Looking back now at everything I did after that day, I realize that I would have missed out on the best days of my program.

After my one day of runner training, I felt like my head was going to explode with information, and I walked away from work super happy. Even better, I had just one more day of work and then two days off. When I went in that morning, I fully expected to still be in Housekeeping. I knew it was going to be a busy day, because the day before the managers had been asking housekeepers with the following day off to come in and work overtime. There were the same few ladies hanging around who always wanted a 6th day to earn overtime or who always asked to "buy rooms" (which means that if the managers have rooms not assigned to anyone's board, but still need to be cleaned, a runner will find a housekeeper—usually someone with an easy or short board—to "buy" the rooms, and they get extra money in their paycheck for doing so).

I walked into the Cast Services building and saw housekeepers everywhere. After I clocked in and walked into the 'assembly hall', I saw one of my friends who told me that ADOs were available and that I should put my name on the list. ADO stands for Approved Day Off. You can get one only by going into work and getting the manager's approval, but if you do get approval, then all the restrictions that come with a sick day are lifted: so you can spend your ADO in the parks, if you want. ADOs are only available when there are too many housekeepers for the amount of boards they have to pass out that day, which seemed silly, since the managers were trying to get people to sign up for overtime the day before. You never know if ADOs will be available on any given day until everyone either turns up for work or calls in sick.

Today, however, there were so many ADOs to be passed out, that I was sent straight home, as did most of my friends. While waiting for the bus (the same one we had just gotten off), we grabbed some breakfast from the canteen to take on the road. I got a sausage muffin—which in England would look like a burger in a scone, but here it is sausage meat formed into the shape of a burger and put into a muffin with the taste and texture of a bread roll.

I continued my fun-filled ADO by changing clothes in the apartment before catching another bus to my favorite park, Hollywood Studios. I was on a mission to spend my ADO drawing, meeting characters, watching the Pixar parade, and attending Fantasmic!

CHAPTER SEVENTEEN

English Buddy

I hadn't heard from Becca for a while, at least not since I had scared her with my stories of Housekeeping and been a bit too negative, but a couple of days after Becca's arrival date I got a message from her. She had found out she was working at Port Orleans and continued the message with "what you have said has made me so nervous." I felt guilty. Even at the time of saying it, I felt bad for scaring her about the role she was going to be working, and I tried to cover it up by saying it might just be my location. Well, that came back to bite me in the backside.

A couple of days later, Becca got on my bus in her uniform. I was so glad have someone British; I loved my new American friends, but it just wasn't the same. I regret not making more of an effort with Becca. I was such a moody bugger because I was really quite resentful that I couldn't be having as much fun at work as my other friends were having. As the time went by, having Becca to work with meant I actually enjoyed myself, and now I kick myself for having taken so long to realize that.

I take pride in being able to help people, and I enjoy having a bit of authority. I really took Becca under my wing. I started to see that she felt just as lonely as I did at the beginning of my program. I made it my mission to make her feel as welcome and as at home as possible, because I knew what it felt like, and I didn't want her to go through what I had.

CHAPTER EIGHTEEN

Towel Animals and Magic Moments

Today I came back from my three days off, fully expecting to be in Housekeeping but secretly excited at the prospect of more runner training ahead of me. Before I'd even had a chance to find two seats for Becca and myself, Leah came over to me and said "You're Runner 2 today." This was an extremely scary concept, since the only time I'd been a runner was with Johnny. I felt unprepared, but I knew I'd pick it up quickly enough, so after I'd finished panicking, I got the keys for my own pargo and went to find where it was parked. When I started it up, I saw that it was low on petrol (gas, sorry!) so my first job was to drive to the gas station at Port Orleans Cast Services.

Suddenly, three ladies stood right in front of my pargo to stop me from driving any farther. They wanted me to take them to their buildings, which is a runners job, but they were all in different buildings, and their pargos hadn't left yet. There were rules in place for the housekeepers, who were supposed to get on only the pargos assigned to their buildings. Some housekeepers chose to ignore the rules and convince themselves that there are quicker ways of getting around the resort. Just ahead, I could see Becca sitting on the curb where her pargo should be; it had left without her. I told the women trying to get on my pargo that I couldn't take them all, as one seat was reserved for Becca. They were ridiculously rude, and so I asked them what building they were going to. "Four," they said. I looked around until I spotted their pargo, still waiting to be filled up with riders. But they continued to sit on my pargo making minimal eye contact and pretending they didn't understand me. This is the one thing I hated the most. They were so selfish, because in the time that I was arguing with them, the driver of their assigned pargo had decided to leave (the runners were aware that the housekeepers ignored the rules). Eventually, they jumped off, without a word to me. Becca ran to take her seat before anyone else could board.

I really enjoyed my first day as a runner on my own. Jill, my manager, said that I could contact her through my radio if I had any questions. I had 16 calls that day, which varied from extra pillows and more shampoo to broken fridges and room re-cleans. Room re-cleans were the worst, because the housekeepers didn't handle me telling them to go back and clean a room very well, and a few them told me that I had to do it.

Some of the intervals between calls were up to an hour long. This is where I got creative. One of the other runners, Marci, had come to join me and Jill in our towel animal escapade. Marci was American, too. She started making some funky things with the foam. Most of the housekeepers would just make animals out of the towels. For the more special guests, or for a guest recovery situation, we could glue glitter, gems, or sequins on them, or make additional items for the animals to wear. This is where I invented the Disney name tag, sorcerer Mickey hat, Peter Pan hat, and the premium Mickey ice cream bar, made with pom poms, foam, and a glue gun. When Leah came from her building, she was rather impressed with my creations.

After making a fairly large army of towel animals, I took some to Becca for her to use. I found her talking to a cute little girl and her mum on their way to the food court for a break from the hot and humid parks. They were staying in one of Becca's rooms, and it was the little girl's birthday.

I feel a Magic Moment coming on…

The girl's favorite character was Shrek, who is not a Disney character, but that didn't stop us. I wished the little girl a magical birthday and told her we'd see her later. I left Becca to continue cleaning her last room and told her to come to the office when she was done. I saw Leah in the office and let her know what I was planning; she wanted to join in. While I made a dog towel animal accessorized with green foam Shrek ears, a Disney name tag with the girl's name on it, and a Mickey ice cream bar, Leah started making a towel birthday cake. We were just putting the final touches to our towel creations and waiting for the glue to dry when Becca walked in. We didn't want the girl's siblings to feel left out of the magic, so Becca took two of my other towel creations to give to them while Leah and I followed with Shrek and the cake creations.

The moment you see the look of amazement on a child's face, and see the mum start to cry because you've gone out of your way to do something extra special for her child, is a moment you will never forget.

CHAPTER NINETEEN

Floating

On June 24, I was back in Housekeeping, but I didn't really mind because I enjoyed having the variety. It was a major checkout day for the resort, with 900 guests checking out and 700 checking in. While I sat in my jumper waiting in fear to get my board, I could see two of the mangers looking at me and clearly having a disagreement. I tried not to make eye contact because I didn't want to get into trouble, but I could tell they were clearly talking about me. Surprisingly enough, I got my board and I only had 3 checkouts. Once I was at my building, I went to see if any of my checkouts had left yet, but they were all still packing up the last of their things so I started on the rooms where the guests had set off early to make the most of their day in the parks. As I went into my first room, I switched on the TV and *Happy Feet* was just starting, so I was tap dancing my way round the room as I cleaned, and it made my day much more enjoyable.

There was one thing I noticed, and the only reason I noticed it was because of a recent incident. Guests decide how much to tip, when to tip, and even *if* to tip their housekeepers. I was classed as a "floater", which meant that I didn't get my own block of rooms. This worked out well for me when I was switching between housekeeping and running, and it's a good system for the housekeepers because they take better care of their assigned rooms, and they're more likely to take pride in their job since it could lead to better tips when they are looking after the same guests throughout their stay. However, on the day of the major check-out, the managers found out that some housekeepers were telling the guests who were staying in their rooms what days they had off. As a result, any floaters, like myself, who would be cleaning these rooms wouldn't get any tips, as the guests knew that it wasn't their housekeeper doing the work.

I learned a valuable lesson. Whenever I'm a guest at a Disney resort, I'll be leaving small tips every day instead of one big tip at the end.

This way, every housekeeper who cleans my room, even the floaters, will get at least some reward.

Today, Amie was working as my manager, and she is so much fun. Amie told me that a couple of the managers don't like me wearing my jumper in the assembly room when I'm waiting for my board (so it turns out I was right, those two managers *were* talking about me). Apparently, they think I wear it while I'm working, and they wanted to report me for it. Amie stuck up for me, and said I only wear it inside before I go to the pargo and take it off when I get to my building, so no guest ever sees me wearing it. Although she stuck up for me, and oddly enough it was a serious issue, she thought it was very funny and had a laugh with me about it.

Amie always made me feel welcome, and it never seemed that she said "hi" just because it would uncomfortable to walk past me in silence. After handing in my board that day, I sat with her in the office and made towel animals. I took out my college program planner to write down some stories from the day for my journal, and I showed her the stickers on the front cover. All of them had come off my board, and it was Amie who had put them on there, just as she put stickers on all the boards when she was managing. They were positive and smiley, and I liked that, so I used to pull them off and keep them. I told her and she thought this was the funniest thing, even more so that no other housekeeper had even mentioned the stickers, as if they didn't really care.

CHAPTER TWENTY

Whistle While You Work

I was runner 1 today, but I always hung out in the office at building one with the managers no matter what running assignment I was given. Celeste was runner 2. Celeste was friends with one of the other lads on the college program, so I had spoken to her before and got along with her quite well. She had never worked before at French Quarter, and during times when neither of us had requests coming in, I practically trained her on being a French Quarter runner. I showed her where the runner room was (this was where they kept all the additional supplies that weren't in the linen rooms), talked her through the different areas of the resort, and told her the lunch times who covered what buildings during those lunch times. She didn't have many calls to start off with, but when she did she sometimes had to radio me to ask me where to find things.

My manager Amie and I were having conversations in song (hence the title of this chapter) just to keep ourselves amused. Then I got four calls in one go, all of them for extra blankets, and while I was on my way to the linen room, Amie called me to say: *"Do you want to go on an adventure?"*

This was a regular occurrence for us. On one of our last adventures, we delivered some special touches to a VIP room. This time, however, it was a mystery. I told Amie that I'd come to her office once I'd finished delivering the blankets. When I got there, she told me that we going to steal linen from building 7 for building 4, which was running low. To make it more fun, we hummed the theme song from James Bond, laughing the whole way. I never thought I'd have so much fun collecting linen from a building.

At 3:30pm, the manager will start collecting the papers of the housekeepers, and then they can go home early, if they're finished. However, Amie had to go to the service building, so she asked me to collect them for her. It felt good being left with this responsibility.

When Amie returned, she came to the office to find me creating towel animals with Celeste, with no calls coming in for either of us. This was quite normal, because after 3:30pm most of the housekeepers had finished their rooms and so they weren't requesting anything extra, and the majority of guests were out in the parks or at the pool. Amie admired all of our creations, then told me she had brought me a present: stickers! I affixed them to my planner, as usual, and saved a few to use in my journal. Amie laughed and said: *"You're like the spoilt child of Housekeeping!"*

CHAPTER TWENTY-ONE

Say "Harry Potter"

There are multiple things that I said throughout my program that I was either asked to:

- Repeat what I said because they didn't hear me;
- Repeat what I said because they want to hear me speak more; or
- Explain what it means.

It was a regular occurrence that when I was asked for the time, no American or Canadian would understand what I told them. There are two common ways to tell the time. The formal way is to say the hour first then the minutes, for example, 9:45 is nine-forty-five. However, the most popular way is to do it the opposite way around and say minutes before hours: 9:45 is quarter to ten. There are multiple possibilities, such as:

- 15 minutes past is quarter past
- 15 minutes to is quarter to
- 30 minutes past is half past

It is no wonder that Americans/Canadians get confused, because if you don't learn to tell the time this way, it will sound very odd when you hear it for the first time. Put it together with a strong British accent and there's a good chance of confusion.

On mornings when Abbie and I both had the day off, we would make pancakes for breakfast, and if it wasn't really early and our roommates were awake, we'd put on some music and have a singa-long. We went through 90s and early 00s bands, which consisted of Busted, McFly, and the Spice Girls. As we were singing "Wannabe", Alexis walked in to the common room and said, "This is brilliant, my British roommates are singing the Spice Girls." Abbie and I really were creating a typical British stereotype for ourselves, but we were enjoying it.

Another time, on the bus coming home from work, there was a group of 6–8 of us, mostly American, but also a Mexican and myself as the lone Brit. Trent, a housekeeper and runner at Port Orleans, kept telling me to say different words, and he'd repeat them to try and replicate my accent. One of the other girls, Talicia, also wanted to try out her English accent, and she wanted to practice with "Harry Potter". For the 45-minute journey home, the two of them would ask me questions where the answer would always be Harry Potter.

CHAPTER TWENTY-TWO

PAC Shift

It was the end of June, and I still hadn't taken full advantage of the opportunities available to me. I had written on my bucket list that I wanted to pick up an extra shift doing something different. I'd heard you could pick up a shift called PAC, which was parade audience control. From what I had read online, you literally control where guests stand to ensure that all fire exits are accessible and walkways are clear. I managed to pick up one shift after several days of checking the extra hours site. Cast members, especially CPs, were keen to get these shifts for two reasons: you got paid to watch the fireworks, and they didn't require any additional training.

I had a confusing start to my PAC shift, as I didn't work in Magic Kingdom and so didn't know my way around the tunnels. I was given directions when I picked up the shift, but I still got confused, and I'm pretty sure I just walked around in a circle the first time. Finally, I made it to the west side of Main Street where the parades set off. I found a cast member, and the only reason I asked him for help is because he were wearing the same costume as me. He was nice enough to radio my manager so I could report in. My job was to control the walkway through the first DEP (Disney's Electrical Parade). I had a wonderful position from which to watch the parade, and I was complimented on my accent every time I spoke. I wish I could have this job all the time.

When the parade ended, I walked up to a group of cast members by the grassy area and was told where to go next. I was going to be working at the first trial of a FastPass prime viewing for Wishes. I was given a Wishes button, a map of the park (as I didn't have one and might need it if a guest asked me for directions), a copy of "Tell-a-Cast" (a cast member leaflet that has information about show times, park hours, and everything you need to know for the week, as well as restroom locations and smoking areas), and finally some Buzz,

Stitch, and Minnie stickers, just in case I wanted to hand them out or use them as part of a magical moment.

The FastPasses for the prime viewing area were randomly handed out to a select number of guests throughout the day. I had to make sure that no one jumped the fence and keep the walkway on the Tomorrowland bridge free for emergency use, but I basically got paid to watch the fireworks with a perfect view.

Toward the end of my shift, a man approached me to ask for directions to the nearest toilet. He then asked me 10 more questions, each one challenging my Magic Kingdom knowledge. At the end I thanked him, wished him a magical evening, and gave my last three stickers to his daughter in the push chair, to which he replied: *I'm sorry, I didn't really need to know any of those answers, I just wanted to hear you talk in that beautiful accent.*

CHAPTER TWENTY-THREE

A Journey to Hundred Acre Wood

For two weeks, Amy, Shauna, and I had been waiting for our character breakfast at Crystal Palace. I got up that morning to start my usual routine, which starts with me going to the bathroom to see whether the toilet lid is down with a Post-it note telling me that it's broken again. Then I'd look through the Post-it notes on the mirror for anything new, and if not, I'd begin painting my face on, as my dad calls it.

With my face painted, I sent a text to the girls. They weren't ready, but told me to come down to their apartment anyway. There was still plenty of time to make our bus. Except we didn't make our bus, and it had nothing to do with getting up late or putting on makeup.

The reason we missed the first bus was a critter that had made its way into Amy and Shauna's room, and taken up lodging on the ceiling right above Amy's bed. Imagine the fear, shock, and pure disgust that Amy felt when she woke up to realize it had been staring at her while she slept. When I got there, they were plotting a way to catch or kill the bugger. Shauna tried spraying it with deodorant, while I constructed a stick out of straws long enough to poke it and dislodge, but it was a rather floppy stick. Despite the floppiness, I managed to poke the thing and it fell to the floor. Amy stuck a glass over the top of it and sprayed more hairspray and deodorant under the glass, then left a note by the glass stating that if anyone was to come in, they were not to move the glass and let the beast escape.

With the critter captured, we were able to head out for the bus. We had our breakfast and met the characters as they did their rounds. Tigger made his way over to our table, and I got so excited that I managed to spill my apple juice everywhere. Tigger saw what happened straight away, and he ran off to the kitchen and came back with a tea towel and a cast member to help clean up the mess I had made.

CHAPTER TWENTY-FOUR

Graduation

While everyone else was in denial about graduation and our program coming to an end, I was really excited. Before we even got our email about graduation I'd decided to ask for some time off and give myself a 3-day holiday before I went home. I got approved for July 31, August 1, and August 2 (which is graduation, with moving out day on the third). I planned to spend my days off buying the last of my souvenirs, taking character photos, riding rides, and seeing my favorite shows: Fantasmic!, Finding Nemo, and Lion King.

On August 1, I went with Amy and Shauna on a "favorite ride day", which included Space Mountain, Expedition Everest, and Soarin'. In between, we went on some of the smaller rides we had done before, such as Living with the Land, where we took pictures of the funky Mickey Mouse-shaped pumpkins. As we got off the ride, Amy reasonably asked: *"Why did we just sit and take pictures of plants?!"*

Graduation took place at Chatham, which makes a lot of sense considering the amount of outdoor space they have. It was due to start at 4pm. We all got dressed up and went to catch the bus together, along with every other CP graduating that day. The bus was hot, sweaty, and packed. You could feel the anger coming from the non-graduating CPs on the bus going to work. Not only wasn't it their day off, but many of them weren't able to get a seat.

When we got to Chatham, we followed the sound of the music. There were queues for many different activities, including receiving your certificate, pictures with Minnie & Mickey in their graduation robes, and pictures with your home flag or adoptive country flag. We went straight for our certificates, which forced us to split up as they were in alphabetical order. Once we had stood in all the lines, we joined in the little dance they had to cheesy tunes spun by a DJ, took loads of group photos, and went to collect more free stuff, especially food. Disney did not stint on the food; there were burgers, pizza, hot dogs, pulled pork, corn, chips, cookies, and brownies. After queuing, dancing, and eating free food in the blazing hot Florida sun, it was time for a costume change before we all headed to Magic Kingdom to watch Wishes together.

All in all, this night was the perfect way to end the program. You really do make friends for life, and you have no idea how much you will miss them until they are taken away from you. I miss getting texts saying "come down", throwing Chinese food on the floor, and self-teaching myself to draw my favorite Disney characters. I miss watching Amy cooking noodles to put in the fridge to take to work and eat them cold the next day. I miss laughing uncontrollably at my obsession with Fantasmic Mickey's entrance dance. I miss watching Paige crying after she told everyone goodbye. I miss hearing her complaining about her "stupid damn ass crackers". I miss frantically packing the night before we are due to move out and go home. I miss going to get energy drinks and brownies at 3am, and bumping into Paige and Leah who were going to catch their flight to New York. I miss our Post-it note conversations. I miss everything! No time will ever compare to this summer, no matter how much I complained, but this isn't goodbye, because:

Goodbye means going away and going away means forgetting.
— J.M. Barrie (*Peter Pan*)

PART TWO
Performing

My second program began on June 10, 2013, and ended on August 16. This time, instead of getting a role I wasn't entirely happy with, I got the role I'd always wanted: character performer.

With every dream, there are high expectations, and for me, my second program didn't hit those high expectations; it went above and beyond.

Editor's Note

As you read this part of the book, you'll come upon something strange. Ema mentions her "friend" Pluto a lot.

Now wait a minute.

Didn't Disney hire Ema to be one of the character performers for Pluto during her college program? Disney did. And isn't this whole second part of the book all about Ema's experiences as Pluto? It is.

So what's with Pluto being her friend?

Disney takes its characters seriously. The term for it is "character integrity", and new cast members who portray characters in the park are told quite clearly, and quite seriously, that *they* are not the characters, because Pluto and his pals really do exist.

But the characters need "friends" to help them do their jobs. And that's where Ema, and all the other cast members in this role at Disney theme parks, come in.

Ema is adamant about upholding character integrity. So, as you read her further adventures, don't expect to find Ema telling you about her experiences as Pluto, even though that's what she's actually telling you about. Ema is Ema, a friend of Pluto, just as all the character performers are not their characters but rather friends of their characters. Ema will be telling you about what her friend Pluto did.

Now that you know the score, let's meet Ema's friend Pluto.

CHAPTER TWENTY-FIVE

Application, Again

The application process for my second program was very different from the first time around. I put in my application on August 29, 2012, and I received my invitation on October 4, 2012, for an interview on the ninth, so it only took four weeks.

I was extremely lucky to get into my first program, as I hadn't even sent in my application before the interviews and just turned up hoping for the best. I wasn't going to do that again. I sat for hours filling in this application; everything seemed so much more in depth. Last year, I did end up filling in an application, but it was after my first interview, I had been offered my second interview and been told they didn't have all my details on file, so would I go fill it out. I wasn't as panicked as I was this year, since now there was so much more riding on an acceptance, and the *right* kind of acceptance. I had my heart set on working in the Entertainment, and I didn't want to give that away. I was so frightened that if I let on that I was only going to be applying for one role, it would be an automatic denial for being inflexible.

The application this year asked questions that I didn't even think about during my interviews last year, such as "What is your motivation for the program?" and "Why do you value cultural exchange and interaction." I was screwed. There was no way I was going to be accepted this year; I didn't even know what to write. I felt like I wrote "I cant wait to share my culture with others and learn about other cultures" over and over again. The whole application form felt like one big repetition of pushing how much I enjoy other people's company. I wrote "culture and spending time with people of different lifestyles has always been a passion of mine" about 5 times, and then I used Microsoft Word's built-in thesaurus to come up with different words that meant the same thing. I should have given my application the title of "I love culture!" in big, bold type.

Finally, I was done and uploaded all the required documents. I scrolled down to the bottom of the screen and found an empty box that I had overlooked. It asked: "Any final comments?"

What on earth do I say here? As if my application wasn't repetitive enough, I had to reconfirm everything I had just said. I needed help! I was not going to let this box be the reason I hang on to my application for another week. The temptation to write "I will offer you my kidney or any other organ I don't need to survive in order to gain a place on this program." Too much? Yeah. I used this space to suck up a little bit more and thank Disney for taking the time to read my disgustingly tedious application. I really should have used the space to apologize in case all of my sucking made them sick.

Interview One

It was the October 4, my birthday, and I was getting excited to celebrate it in style with a Disney-themed fancy dress night out at university. That morning my phone had started going crazy with Facebook notifications from the Disney ICP 2013 group. People were getting their first interview invitation emails. My heart stopped for a moment. I was so scared, and I felt like I was going to faint. I checked my email account. The screen said "updating mail..." for what felt like an hour, but was actually less than 30 seconds. The result? No new mail. I was devastated. How come other people were getting their invitations before me? Am I even getting a first interview?

I started receiving texts from my friends (who had been with me on the program the year before). They had received their invitations and wanted to know if I'd be at the Liverpool interviews, too. I couldn't even reply. This was it. My Disney dream was over before it had begun. I sat in my room for a little while and then decided I'd start re-arranging my things and cleaning in preparation for my amazing 21st birthday party and dressing up as Rapunzel.

I plugged my phone into my speakers, put the music on full volume, and sang at the top of my voice to *Glee* soundtrack: "Why do I reach for the stars, when I don't have wings to carry me that far..." As the music faded, I heard a *ding*. Email!

I launched myself at my phone and clicked on the mail icon. The subject line read: "The Disney Summer Work Experience". I clicked open and before the screen had fully loaded I'd closed my eyes and crossed my fingers. I took a deep breath, gave myself a little pep talk (in my head), and peered out of one eye to see a location and date/time highlighted in yellow. To be honest, I don't remember much else about that email other than the important bits highlighted. I rang my parents to tell them straight away. I was so excited to have a chance to sell myself and prove that I'm worthy of a second summer at Disney World.

After going through the ordeal of waiting for the email, the interview seemed fairly straightforward and simple, especially in comparison to my first-year interview where I felt like I was fighting to speak against the other twenty people, but this year it was groups of ten.

On October 9, at 5:59am, I woke up with butterflies in my stomach, I sat bolt upright on my bed. Then my alarm went off a minute later. It was time to start getting ready before I called a taxi to take me to the train station. I had planned to get the train with my friend Leah, who had participated in the program the year before with me, working at the Polynesian's 'Ohana restaurant. We met up with Abbie (who had worked at French Quarter in quick service), my roommate from the previous year, and also Charlie (who had worked at the Polynesian in Custodial). We had all sat together in a small lecture hall at Liverpool John Moores University, and so they put us all in the same interview group, which made me feel a lot more at ease, even though I wasn't really that nervous to start with.

We had started the day at 7am to get the train to Liverpool and arrived at 9 for the 9:30 presentation. They tell you to stay seated while they come round and give you an interview slot (this year I had 12:30pm), and then you are allowed to go explore the city, get some food, and do some shopping, until you need to return for your group interview. We had already grabbed some snacks from the Tesco Express on the walk up to the interview building, so none of us were particularly hungry, but we all agreed that we would go to Nandos after the interview for a late lunch. I love Nandos, and so this was all I was thinking about before the interview; it kept my mind off it, and it wasn't as if I needed to think about what I wanted to eat, because I always order the same thing: lemon-and-herb chicken burger, with garlic bread, chips, and halloumi cheese.

Last time, the interviews (I was told) had gone as late as 8pm, but this year no one had a slot past 5:30pm. I'm not sure if that is because there were less applicants or more interviewers, but it didn't really matter. The interview itself, like last time, was held in a group setting, with 10–15 applicants in each group. Everyone was given a chance to answer every question, unlike before. There were only 10 people in my group, and 4 of us had come from the same university. Another member of my group was Abbie, my former roommate. We were asked a number of different questions, including:

- Why do you want to work for Disney?
- Do you have any tattoos or piercings?
- Give an interesting fact about yourself?
- How would you deal with the heat?
- How would you deal with difficulties arising from roommates and homesickness?
- How would you deal with different cultures?
- Describe your hometown in one word or sentence?
- How would you respond to certain scenarios: Mine was that the character had to go in so you closed the queue, but a family wanted to see him.
- Give an example of good guest service that you have provided or received.
- How will the program help you in later life?
- Which character are you most like?

And because I've done the program before, I got asked: What would I have done differently if I could re-start my first program?

A key thing I noticed is that they watched for how you interacted within social situations and large groups. Obviously, they do not want a shy cast member, nor do they want a rude cast member who interrupts and cuts people off mid-sentence without an apology just to make their point or get attention. I could see that the recruiters were watching how we interacted with one another, but really they were assessing our personalities.

I did feel myself start to suck up and praise everything about the Disney Company, but then pulled back when I realized that being a suck up just wasn't me. I love Disney, and that totally is me, but I am also a bunch of other things, and while I was fan-girling over the creative ideas the Imagineers have come up with, I was hiding all my other amazing qualities that I wanted to showcase to the recruiters. I came back to being myself, and in those few seconds that I chose to do this, I realized that if I didn't get a second interview, then they didn't like the true me, so it would be for the best.

Interview Two

October 25, 2012. I had to travel to Liverpool again. This time, I had a full 9 hours of sleep, did not wake up once during the night, and felt refreshed and confident when the alarm went off at 6:00am. I phoned my taxi and sat patiently on the bottom step in my university house. I saw some flickers of light, jumped up, and ran to open the door, assuming it was my taxi, but the driver went straight past the house. It wasn't my taxi. I checked the time on my phone. 6:35am. I began to panic and thought about ringing the taxi company. How stupid that would have been: it's only been five minutes since I called them in the first place.

As I stood in the open doorway, I saw the same car that had just driven past. It was now coming back the other way, slowly. He's got to be looking for my house, I thought. Just then, my phone rang with a Chester area code. It was the taxi driver. Hurrah!

At this time of the morning, my usually energetic, bubbly self hasn't fully emerged, and I don't like talking to people so early in the day. But the driver had obviously been awake for hours, and he wanted to talk. He was telling me stories from his past fares, in particular the one about the university students who'd dropped their takeaway pizza on the dirty sidewalk but picked it up and put it back in the box before they climbed into his cab.

I think he realized I wasn't listening to his stories, and so he decided to engage me in conversation, instead. Luckily, we were almost at the train station by then. He asked me if I was a nurse going on placement, because there would be "no other sane reason for you to be awake and dolled up this early." I tried my hardest to be polite, but I didn't have the energy for anything more than: "I have a job interview." He wasn't satisfied. "Oh, well it must be a really important company to you to have you awake at this hour." I get it, it's early, I do have a clock, but I kindly replied with, "Yes, it is kind of a dream of mine." And then we were pulling up at the train station. I gave him money for the fare and he wished me a sincere "good luck, go get your dream." I smiled and said "thank you" as genuinely as I could muster.

Once inside the station, I quickly I found Leah and we boarded the train for Liverpool, arriving on time at John Moores University where we sat through more presentations and more PowerPoints. This time, however, it was different, because the presentations were delivered by Disney recruiters, whose accents made me miss America even more.

They started off with introductions all around and then collected our paperwork, which included:

- Two photocopies of the main passport page
- Actual passport
- Birth certificate
- Proof of home address
- CV
- Proof of student status
- Completed university accreditation letter (you are given the template in the email, which your university lecturer must complete and sign)
- Completed role checklist
- Chosen date period for the program

The recruiters then gave me my time slot for the interview and made sure that none of the information on my form had changed. They also asked how I would like my name spelled on my nametag. My name is officially "Emma", but I prefer "Ema". There are many reasons for this, not the least of which is that Emma is a common name and during my teen-aged rebellion phase I decided that I wanted to be more unique, and so dropped an "m". I wasn't bold enough to change my name completely. In school, I wasn't a cool kid, or in with the popular crowd, so I needed to do something subtle, something that would go unnoticed by all but my closest friends, who would think it cool. Or at least that's what I tell people when they ask about the missing "m". As long as your nickname is Disney-appropriate, they're happy to put it on your nametag in place of your given name.

In addition, the recruiter asked me what location I wanted on my name tag. You can specify your place of birth, where you live now, where your parents live, where you went to university, anything reasonable, really. I chose the name of a bigger town about 20 minutes from where I live, since few enough Brits know the name of my little town, and so it's highly doubtful that any Americans would have heard of it. I don't even live exactly in that little town. I should have asked them to put "In the middle of fields, England" on my nametag, which is more accurate, but Disney doesn't appreciate that kind of humor.

CHAPTER TWENTY-SIX

Acceptance, Again

I walked into the interview room to be greeted by Jane, a small woman with an American accent. She made me feel at ease right away, but I still couldn't shake the premonition that this year wouldn't be as lucky for me as last year, especially since I had ticked only one role (performer) on my application. If I couldn't have that role, I decided, then I didn't want the program.

I sat down on a chair facing a desk with a pile of documents from other interviewees on one side and my documents spread out in front of Jane. She had spent 5 minutes going through them before inviting me into the room. First impressions are crucial, and Jane's first impression of me was that ridiculous application with all the cultural happy-talk I had written. She wasted no time getting right to it: "You have only ticked one box?"

I felt my heart sink. "Yes, I know it makes me come across completely inflexible, but I really want this role, and I hope that it shows my determination and passion for the Entertainment department." She reminded me that PhotoPass and attendant are also Entertainment roles, so why was I fixated on performer?

I could have rambled on for hours and hours about my love for Disney and performing and how it would be a dream come true to be a performer at Walt Disney World. But I didn't. I kept my answers short and to the point, and tried not to come off as insincere.

Jane gave no clue as to whether my answers were what she wanted to hear. Before I knew it, the interview was over, and I was out the door.

Two weeks later. I had turned off Facebook group notifications as I was having heart palpitations whenever my phone buzzed thinking that it would be from someone who had gotten their acceptance, and then someone else, and then someone else, but never me.

Fortunately, I was plenty pre-occupied with reading for my dissertation and getting ready to leave university for home. I had a week away from school. My dad had offered to come pick me up so I wouldn't have to lug thirty research books, a laptop, and a suitcase full of clothes onto the train. As soon as I arrived back home, I set up my laptop and got busy printing articles, highlighting, researching, printing more articles, and forgetting about Disney.

After hours of this, I decided to take a break and automatically went to Facebook. I'd turned off my group notifications, but I was still getting comments in my feed. And there they were: people bragging about their acceptances to the college program.

I dropped my phone and went straight to my laptop to check my emails. It would have been quicker to use my phone, but I wasn't thinking clearly. I squinted my eyes at the screen, afraid to see whatever was—or more importantly, was not—there. But still I saw it, amid my four new emails: Disney!

I had gotten an email, but lacked the courage to open it. I stared at it. I'd already told my family, my friends, and my boyfriend how well the interview had gone, and they probably assumed that my acceptance was a given. What would I tell them if it there wasn't an acceptance?

I opened the email and saw red—literally. The text was in red. Nothing good is ever printed in red ink, and so I immediately thought the worst. Then I saw it:

CONGRATULATIONS!

You have been offered a place on Disney's J-1 Cultural Exchange Program.

Your role in the show will be Character Performer.

Red. My new favorite color.

CHAPTER TWENTY-SEVEN

Everything in Between

In March, I received my Disney information pack. I needed to ring the embassy straight away if I wanted to get my first choice of a visa appointment time.

I went through the same procedure as the year before, arranging all my necessary paperwork on the floor in front of me. I dialed the embassy and told the lovely woman who answered that phone number that I needed a visa for Disney's college program, which I'd also done the year before. Since I was applying for the same category of visa within the span of 12 months, I didn't have to physically go to the embassy if I didn't want to, which as I live at the other end of the country, was definitely music to my ears. I still had to pay their fees and fill out their forms, but at least I wouldn't have to pay for a train and sit for hours in their waiting room for them to see me.

The next day, March 26, I rang the courier to have my stuff collected. They said they'd stop by anywhere from 6am to 8pm the following day. This meant I had to get up super early, and as I was in the house alone, I soon got super bored. I had to sit near the front door so I wouldn't miss their knock. At 9:35am, a woman arrived in a normal-looking car and announced herself as from the courier service. I was kind of skeptical handing over sensitive documents to a random woman in a regular car when I was expecting a courier van and a representative in uniform. However, she showed me an envelope with the courier logo printed on the side, and I had to take the receipt for the courier service out of my pile of documents and put everything else inside the envelope. She sealed it in front of me and asked me to sign for it, and off she went.

CHAPTER TWENTY-EIGHT

DORMS

On April 18, 2013, Disney released a post online that sent the ICP Facebook group crazy. Disney was changing our living experience on the program. Before now, we had been allocated housing and had no say in who we wanted to live with. However, American participants could select their roommates and housing complex preference. Disney had seen how successful it had been with the American participants, and so decided to offer the same perk to international participants.

I knew right away that I wanted to be Amy's roommate; I just didn't know if she wanted to be mine. It was 3 days after the news had come out, and I was thinking of a way to bring the roommate idea up with her. It was as nerve-wracking as asking someone out on a date. After discussing our preferences for housing complexes and the benefits of living at Vista with all the shops right on your doorstep, it seemed that we were in agreement on housing. The conversation continued:

> Amy: Are you gonna request to live with someone who you met last year?
>
> Ema: Well, all my friends who are going back are over 21, and two of them arrive on the 3rd, but they all want to live in an over-21 apartment, so I don't know what to do.
>
> Amy: Aww, well, we could always request to be together?
>
> Ema: Yes!! I would love that.
>
> Amy: Getting excited again now!

The pre-registration started in May 2013, and all we knew was that we would receive an email 10 days before our arrival date and could then fill in our pre-registration. It wasn't until May 29 when the first wave of emails were sent out. Amy got hers first, and mine closely followed. The first thing Amy said was: "Right, how do we do it?"

We each set up an account in DORMS. This part took *forever*. I fell at the first hurdle. We got two emails, one with the instructions and the link to follow to start the process and the other with a temporary password that we could use until we reset it during registration. I swear that resetting my password was the world's most difficult struggle, much tougher than deciding what to eat for lunch some days. So many rules and restrictions! Rule number 1: Your password can't contain words from the dictionary. WHAT?! Am I just supposed to throw a load of letters together and hope I remember it. The next problem was that, as far as I'm aware, proper names aren't in the dictionary. But, according to the registration form, proper names *are* in the dictionary, and so you can't have those, either. I snuck around the system by taking a few letters from my first name and my last and then added a load of numbers on the end. I wrote my newly created password down in a bunch of different place so I wouldn't lose it and get locked out of my account.

Finally, we both made it to the section which would require us to link our applications so we could room together. Amy inputted my roommate number, and then I had to wait until the system let me accept her invitation. It was a bit like accepting a friend request on Facebook. After a few minutes of waiting, it came through, I accepted it, and that was that. Amy was never going to be able to escape me now, unless Disney put me in a box somewhere for the mutual good.

CHAPTER TWENTY-NINE

Arrival, Again

After spending 9 hours trapped on a plane, being very indecisive about what movies to watch, and actually making a decision to turn *Les Miserables* off and watch season 2 of *Hannah Montana* instead, it was safe to say I was exhausted and my brain was no longer functioning. I had been awake 14 hours, and it was only 3:20pm. I didn't start traveling the day before, so how was it still so early in the day? Time difference. This was a major problem for everyone aboard that plane. We had got on our 9-hour flight at 11 o clock this morning, and it was the middle of the day when we landed. It confused me last year, and it confused me just as much this year.

I just wanted to sleep, but I knew if I did, then I'd be worse off, and my body's clock even more out of joint. Amy and I decided that this time we wouldn't do the dreaded food shop at Walmart, which is what everyone does when they first arrive, but instead we'd get just enough supplies for the next few days at the nearby Walgreens and then hit Walmart later, when it wouldn't be so packed with College Program kids stocking up on the stuff they thought they'd need (but which they often didn't need).

First, though, we had to collect our housing paperwork and find out where we'd be staying. Last year, I didn't know what to expect, and so had no reason to get nervous; this year, the pressure was on. Amy and I wanted to be in the same apartment. Whether Disney wanted that, too, was something we'd soon learn.

Even though I was over 21 on this program, and eligible to stay in an apartment with others my age and not worry about Disney terming us for alcohol, I decided not to do that. Few of my friends back home understood my decision, but I hadn't come here to drink and to watch my roommates drink. This was my chance, probably my once-in-a-lifetime chance, to be a performer at Disney World, and I wasn't going to blow it. Many of the people I met last year had no interest in working for the company, and they acted like it—adding alcohol to that attitude would only make it worse. I didn't want to share a room with a girl who brought back a new guy every night or who slugged from a bottle of gin every chance she got. Being in a wellness apartment took away the gin, at least, and besides, Amy wasn't over 21 and wouldn't be able to stay in an alcohol-friendly apartment.

The friendly Disney lady at the counter where I turned in my paperwork asked about my flight and whether I was excited to be back here. Then she handed me an envelope full of documents and wished me a magical day. I frantically opened my envelope to find my apartment complex and number.

Chatham Square, #21204.

So it wasn't Vista Way, like we had requested, but it was a new program, and it seemed fitting that I would get to enjoy this new journey in a new complex. I was just hoping that Amy had the same apartment number.

I waited and watched as she chatted to the cast member who had her envelope. Finally, she took it and ran over to me.

Ema: What have you got?

Amy (disappointed): Chatham.

Ema: That's okay, because I did, too. Are we together? What's your apartment number?

Amy: 21204.

CHAPTER THIRTY

Tangled Up in the Bedsheets

We had taken our seats after grabbing a handful of freshly baked cookies and a bottle of water. Next to us was a girl, Katie, whom I had sat next to on the plane. She was a dancer from Sheffield. We instantly connected over our love of musicals, and she had told us she was going to be a performer, too. We had chatted quite a bit in the departure lounge at the airport. So she came to sit with us to eat cookies while we waited for the presentation to start. I asked her where she was going to be living. Chatham! She had requested to live with someone, too, but they were coming in on the London flight and hadn't arrived yet. I told her we were also in Chatham so we could meet up before all the orientation meetings, I asked for her apartment number. 21204!

Can you believe it? Three performers under one roof. This was going to be the best summer ever.

At this moment, I heard a friendly American voice and turned around to see Mickey standing there, the man who had helped me the year before. I gave him the biggest smile and he smiled back and waved I couldn't wait to tell him that I had gotten my dream job. But first, we had to sit through a video presentation and a mini-introduction to the program. It was the same presentation video we had watched the year before, and to be honest, I already knew what it was like to be in the program. It was a new year and things may have changed, but I was so excited to be living with Amy and Katie, and just being back here, that I couldn't concentrate.

When the presentation was over, it was time to go find our suitcases that had been unloaded from the taxi and piled up in the corner. For those of us who weren't living in Vista, we were told to get our luggage and board the mini bus for our designated complex. I went with Amy, Katie, Vicki (another girl who would also be living with us), and a few others living in Chatham, including Sarah Smiles. Sarah won the legacy award, the highest of the cast member awards, which means that you are truly fantasmic, and entitles you to a blue nametag so everyone knows it. The bus ride to Chatham helped me learn how this girl lives up to her name of Sarah Smiles, because she has a phobia to silence and really does smile, a lot. Whenever conversation lapsed, she would pick it up with a spiel about our favorite parks and characters, films, housing complexes, things to do outside of Disney, where the best shops are, what food we have to try, and everything else imaginable. She did get us all talking, and by the time we got off the bus we were no longer as awkward toward one another as we had been when we got on. I suppose that was the point.

Our apartment was in the back left-hand corner of the complex, with a view of Patterson Court, one of the other complexes. We opened our front door and saw a flight of stairs, an unusual layout for a Disney apartment. We dragged our mountain of luggage up the stairs, and once in the apartment proper we found other suitcases that had already been unpacked. We had roommates. But none of them were in. They must have arrived on an earlier flight, which meant they weren't British because our plane was the first one from England to land in Orlando that day.

Amy and I found a room where both beds were free and grabbed it. My bed was pushed up next to the window. We had a shared bathroom which joined two rooms, and we walked through to find Katie and Vicki setting up camp. I knew I had to get my bed made first, because if we went out I wouldn't want to do it when I got back, and it makes me feel more at home. I opened my suitcase and rooted around the mountain of clothes and shoes to find my bedding and covers. And that leads into another story.

As I'm going through my suitcase, Amy is unpacking clothes and finding places for all her bits and bobs around our room. She had started to organize her make up on the dresser while I was putting sheets on my mattress and pillowcases on my pillows. All I had left to do was the duvet. This is always a challenge for any British person, but add jet lag and it can become even more confusing. I find the easiest way to put covers on my duvet is to turn the covers inside out, grab the corners of the duvet, shake the covers until they assume the right position, and then just pull the duvet up to the other two corners and do up the poppers at the bottom. My usual approach went completely tits up, as I grabbed the wrong corners and put the duvet in a landscape position on a portrait cover.

Logic told me that the easiest way to sort out the mess was to get into the cover and move the duvet around while I was inside my sheets. I did this all without thinking that Amy might find it funny at best and weird at worst. She burst into laughter. I asked what she'd done, not realizing that I was asking from within my bedsheets. "It's you," she said, "what are you doing inside your duvet?" At that point, I realized that what I was doing was insane, and burst into fits of laughter myself. Amy said, " I have to take a picture." In one of our many pre-Disney conversations, we had promised each other to take as many photos as possible to document the entire summer, as well as videos for vlogs. Amy kept her promise. From this moment on, I knew we would be the best of friends, and I can understand now how so many people thought we knew each other from home.

CHAPTER THIRTY-ONE

Dole Whip

Katie and Vicki decided to head out to Walmart, while Amy and I made the less sensible choice of taking a bus to the Polynesian to meet my roommate from last year, Abbie, for Dole whip. As we were all getting ready to leave, we heard a male and a female voice coming up the stairs. Another of our roommates had arrived, with her dad in tow. "Hi, I'm Marley," she said, in a friendly voice.

Marley was from Port Orange, about an hour's drive north of Disney World. I was automatically jealous that she lived so close to the happiest place on earth. Her dad told Marley how lucky she was to be living with British girls. She said she was going to get some things with her dad that she had forgotten, and we said we were going to Polynesian and that she was welcome to join us later.

As it turned out, we didn't go anywhere, but became distracted with unpacking all of our luggage and checking out all the cupboards in the apartment. Katie came across a bottle of milk in the fridge. We began talking about Marley, wondering what she'd be like as a roommate, and Katie kept referring to her as Molly. Confused, I said:

Ema: Who's Molly? I thought her name was Marley.

Katie: Marley?

Ema: Yeah, like *Marley & Me*.

Katie: It says Molly on this bottle of milk in the fridge.

We all burst out laughing. I'd even saved her in my phone as Marley.

CHAPTER THIRTY-TWO

Roommate Bonding

On the day after our orientation, Amy and I decided that it was finally time to go to Walmart to buy some food that we could actually assemble into a meal. We had been living off Lunchables and cookies and a lot of fizzy drinks from the vending machine.

The most logical way to prepare for your first trip to Walmart is to make structured a list of all the essentials so you don't get home and realize you've missed something you desperately needed. Neither of us did this; instead, we sat with our phones on the bus to Walmart trying to think of what we needed and typing it into a message. Amy's list started off with cookies, truly a needful thing.

At Walmart, we bypassed the food aisles and headed straight to cosmetics and crafts. It took us an hour to start putting food in our cart, because first we had to look at all the Disney clothes and pins and tacky touristy Florida gifts that Walmart sells. I bought some giant colored felt tips pens to use for writing messages to one another back at the apartment.

By this time, I was starting to get hungry, and bags and bags of amazing American treats found their way into our trolley. We did get the essentials, as well: bread, rolls, butter, smoothies, pancake mix. At the frozen aisle, we added pizzas and tater tots.

Back at the apartment, we found all the roomies chilling in front of a giant TV watching Netflix. We didn't have a TV set last year, because everyone in the apartment had flown to Orlando and there was no room for a TV in our luggage. Having American roommates certainly did come with advantages.

As I put away my food and placed my felt tips on the table, Merrite, an extremely bubbly girl from Minnesota who could give Sarah Smiles a run for her money, said she had a good idea of something we could do with my pens. She got us all some paper and said we had to write down information about ourselves. This was a really cute idea, and obviously the questions were focused around Disney, so favorite Disney film, park, ride, princess, villain. And of course, the basics, too: the basics, name, where we were from, our role. We stuck our finished information sheets to the pin board in the communal area. It was already starting to feel like home.

CHAPTER THIRTY-THREE

Welcome to Entertainment

Friday, June 14. It's time for my first department training class. Up until now, I've learned the exact same things they taught me last year, but this class was brand new. Welcome to Entertainment! It was a whirlwind of a class. I thought, living with three other girls who were also in Entertainment, that I'd be in the class with at least one of them. No such luck.

I already had the job, but Disney could take it away from me if I didn't pass my training. This class wasn't a do-or-die, but I still felt nervous and had those familiar butterflies in my stomach that everyone gets in advance of an audition. Proper training hadn't even begun, and already I was a wreck.

I took the bus from Chatham and bumped into a few girls from England who were going to be attendants. I knew they must have been in the same class as me, since they were wearing their professional attire with their nametags on. We all piled on the bus with the massive group of college programmers dressed in a variety of crazy costumes.

At Disney, we don't have the sort of uniforms you would wear to work anywhere else; here, everyone calls them "costumes", and work is a "show" with your workplace "onstage". Much of the terminology you would hear in the theater is used at Disney theme parks. Some of the costumes are theatrical indeed, such as the old-fashioned dresses worn by the "fairy godmothers" at Bibbiti Bobbidi Boutique. We were all jealous of those.

My Entertainment training was being held at a place called DAK WARDROBE/DISNEY UNI. We clocked in for the first time, at 8am, after meeting wonderful, energetic people who had no business being so wonderful and energetic that early in the morning. We had two trainers, both of them male. One of them, Rafael, had just been nominated for the legacy award (that blue nametag I told you about earlier). He had worked as a PhotoPass photographer for most of this time with the company, but had recently transferred here.

The instructors know the safety stuff is necessary but boring, and so they try to get it out of the way first so we can finish with the fun stuff. Only Disney can make learning about safety not entirely dull, even when the lesson is how to pick up a heavy item.

The class began with a few basic rules. Number one, no matter what your role, and this does extend outside the Entertainment department, character integrity is essential to the magic. Unfortunately, there are people who like to spoil the magic for others in order to gain a sense of "I know more than everyone else", which I find pathetic. Everyone who comes to work for Disney understands and accepts the rules, and if you chose to break them and spoil experiences for other cast members who still hold onto the magic they knew as children, you shouldn't work for Disney.

We spent quite awhile going over the importance of this rule, and the only reason it takes so long is because if it isn't emphasized enough, some people don't seem to get it.

Next, we went to hear all about the green, yellow, and red zones of lifting. The instructors thought it an important lesson, but I never once used these techniques during the entire course of my program. But at least I had the skills to safely execute a good lift if I was required, because:

SAFE D BEGINS WITH ME!

We talked a lot about how the Entertainment department is completely different from every other department on Disney property, because people are always looking for ways to "break" it. For examples, some guests think it's cool to ask Pluto whether he has air vents or fans inside his costume. Pluto doesn't speak, and so he signs back confusion. He's a dog, not a human, and so he's supposed to be confused. He'd probably like to say that even dogs are smart enough to know that they don't have fans inside their heads. That's why attendants are always close by to help the non-speaking characters like Pluto. A good attendant will know what a character would be expected to say, but can't.

At this point, we received our role-based training schedule. Rafael said that some of the schedule needed explaining, so he brought us up to the front in small groups to do so, with the groups then split based on roles. We were told that at some point during training we would have a "realization moment" when we would truly understand the amazing impact of what we do, and that we have to power to make a guest's day very special.

From Disney University we boarded the West Clock bus, which is the bus that all cast members use to travel back and forth to Disney University, Magic Kingdom Costuming, the Magic Kingdom cast parking lot, and Cast Connections. Most everyone who works at the Magic Kingdom uses this bus to get to work. We all piled on.

At Magic Kingdom, we went on a mini tour of the tunnels, which are really the ground floor of the park, with everything else built on top of them on the second floor. Using these tunnels, cast members can pop up in their work location without having to walk through another land and spoil the magic. It's why you never see a cowboy in Tomorrowland.

With our tour complete, we had lunch in the Mouseketeria, the cast member cafeteria in the tunnels. Imagine a high school cafeteria, and you'll have a decent idea of what it looks like. Cast members in and out of costume grab meals here. You might see Maleficent gobbling some mac-and-cheese, or Cinderella chowing down on a hamburger, or even Donald Duck slurping some sesame noodles. In some ways, it's the *Star Wars* cantina right here on earth.

On the bus back to Disney University, we watched a montage video with testimonials from cast members and guests about the entertainment at Disney. Then Rafael read us a letter from a guest who had written to the PhotoPass department to thank them for taking a picture of her and her sister. I am getting chills just thinking of this story...

These sisters fought like hell and couldn't agree on a single thing. One day, they had a massive argument and stopped speaking to each other. The parents tried everything. In the meantime, they had both started families, and neither had met the other's children. The parents decided to plan a trip to Disney World for all of them, so they secretly told each sister that they were just going with them. Of course, the sisters uncovered the lie when they saw one another during check-in, but if they were ever going to settle their differences, it would be here. They had the best holiday and forgot about everything they'd ever fought about. They bought matching Minnie ears and got a picture of just the two of them on Main Street before the rest of the family piled in to join them for another picture. Two weeks after the vacation finished, one of the sisters was in a car accident and passed away. The other sister had written to PhotoPass to thank them for taking the final picture of the two of them, as without it the surviving sister would have had no recent picture of them together.

If you aren't sobbing, your heart is made of stone.

There hasn't been a single moment, not one, that I felt I'd made the wrong decision in coming back here again. So far, the program was living up to expectations, unlike last year. I would have been gutted if I'd had to spend another summer hating my job.

CHAPTER THIRTY-FOUR

Character Training

In addition to the Welcome to Entertainment class, I also had to take part in four days of performer training. Again, as I lived with two other performers, I thought we might have been lucky enough to attend training as a group, but I was wrong. Unlucky me. Amy and Katie were scheduled together for the four days, and I was going to be on my lonesome. They started training the day before me, but refused to divulge any of the details because they didn't want to spoil it.

Finally, it came my turn.

The first two days of training consisted of indoor-based activities. I was in a group of ten: five Americans, four Brits, and one French. As we waited outside the Animal Kingdom, our trainers (Toni, Jimmy, and Adam) pulled up in a van and drove us around to the back of the building where our training would begin.

We spent the first part of the day going over the motto that every Disney cast member remembers: SAFE D BEGINS WITH ME. It begins with me because I put into practice all the important health and safety rules that Disney teaches me, like the correct way to pick up a box. Even as performers we have to embrace the safety rules. If you ever meet someone who has been a performer, or you work at Disney and you think that the performers have caught a few breaks, we haven't: we learn the same basics as everyone else, and we have to embed the safety rules into our day, too.

As is the case with most training, the first day was relatively dull and uneventful. Disney likes to get the less interesting aspects of the course out of the way as quickly as possible.

On day two, after an appearance by Mr. Smee, who wished us luck and then went in search of a certain ticking croc, we "met" some of the characters to which we'd been assigned (in Disney-speak, we were going to "hang out with our friends") and began to learn their habits. We had to learn what the character likes, how it acts, whether it prefers to walk or run, sleep or play, etc. My "friend", Pluto, shows a lot of energy and moves around enthusiastically, so part of the preparation for becoming "friends" with Pluto in advance of beginning my role onstage was to learn how he behaves.

On day three, we were ready to venture into the park and meet guests with our new "friends" for the first time. We all went to Epcot for the day (and for day four, as well) and were given a mini-tour of the Epcot Cast building before gathering at the Entertainment base. It's strange when you are walking around backstage, because you can never guess which ride or show is on the other side of the wall.

We were then given yet another tour, this time of the Entertainment department, and told how the system works and the schedules that performers must keep:

Stage 1: Clock in. Every cast member can clock in 15 minutes before their shift starts; failure to clock in or turn up to work results in a point on your record. College program participants can rack up no more than 3 points every 30 days before facing consequences, including termination, which for an international means leaving the country within 24 hours. If you don't, your name will go on a "black list" and might bar you from returning here in future, even on a tourist visa.

Stage 2: Report to the duty captain in their office at the Entertainment building. At some parks, you have to report to a different duty captain depending on where you are performing; for example, Magic Kingdom is the base for all character dining at the Contemporary, Grand Floridian, and Polynesian resorts. Once you've reported in and have told the duty captain where you'll be performing, and with which character, they tick you name off the list and your day begins.

Stage 3: Get into your basics, which are the clothes given to you by the Entertainment department to wear while performing. Attire is kept simple to keep performers cool and comfortable throughout the day.

We had these three stages drilled into our heads during the final two days of our training. After we had completed our stages, we began our warm-ups. It takes a lot of energy to dance and jump around and do whatever it is your character likes to do. Warm-up sessions vary by character, and Disney provides documentation of the best exercises for each character, based on how much energy the character expends and what body parts it uses most. Tigger, for example, does a lot of bouncing, and so his warm-up consists of leg exercises.

Pluto always brought out the best in me. I love his energy, but also how caring and compassionate he is toward kids. He knows how to make their day, and it helps that all of the guests love Pluto and are excited to see him.

CHAPTER THIRTY-FIVE

DinoLand USA

After four days of training and my first day of work, I felt ready to go out into the Disney parks and perform. My assigned area was DinoLand USA in the Animal Kingdom. I couldn't remember ever having met Pluto there, but maybe that's because my family never cared much for that section of the park.

My meet-and-greet spot featured both Pluto and Goofy. I arrived at the Entertainment building and followed two very tall lads to the duty manager's office. I was ready to just get on with it and go find Pluto, but as I walked in and said "Hi" the duty manger's face lit up. "Are you British?" I had made his day. Apparently, there aren't many British performers, and this guy had an obsession, I would call it, with England and its royal family.

My partner, who was "friends" with Goofy, was French. I have nothing against any other culture; in fact I used this program to embrace as many different cultures as possible and to learn new things (just as I'd written numerous times on my application!). The French guy was new and not much of a conversationalist. No matter how much I tried to interact with him, his answers to my questions were usually limited to "yes" or "no". Eventually, I moved away to meet some of the other people in the very large break room (so large that it came with its own toilets, sofas, TV, and box of VHS tapes). The character attendants, most of them full-time cast members, were extremely nice and happy to answer my questions.

My day was spent mostly with a never-ending stream of cute kids. One little girl dressed as Belle curtsied to Pluto, so of course Pluto bowed in return. Her dad captured it on film, and I heard the mother remark that Pluto was the first character to bow to her daughter after the curtsy. Pluto signed some challenging items with his clumsy paws, including a scrap of paper no bigger than the palm of my hand, a hat (which would have been fine if Pluto hadn't been handed a 2-inch crayon to sign it with), and park maps (a free substitute for Disney's pricey autographs books). By the way, Pluto hates signing park maps unless they're on a clipboard or a hard, flat surface.

During my first week of work, I was at DinoLand every day. I was disappointed, since my friends had scored much more interesting (and more "Disneyish") locations. But as soon as I had spent my first day in DinoLand, I took it all back. It was a great place to hang out.

On my third day, I experienced my first 12-hour shift. I'd be the first to arrive in DinoLand and the last to leave. I met a cast member who'd been there for the past couple of days, but who had kept mostly to himself and hadn't said much. He was a full-time and a "force bid" in DinoLand. All full-time cast members have to bid on a location and don't receive a schedule like mine (which is described as "global", because I'm able to work anywhere). Unfortunately, the high demand for some locations means that cast members have to bid for them, a very complex system that I never did fully understand. What I did understand was that most cast members didn't like force bidding, as it put some of the less successful ones in less desirable locations.

The most magical memory of the day for me involved a dad and his daughter. The dad had a plush Eeyore under his arm, and like every dad at Disney World, had clearly been forced to carry it after his child had demanded to take it into the park that day and then gotten tired of holding it. Since the Eeyore was roughly ball shaped, Pluto became interested in a game of catch with it. He took Eeyore while the girl was greeting Goofy and balanced it on his large snout. The girl burst out laughing as her dad snapped a photo.

In my training, I had been taught how Pluto behaved, and for the first time I felt as if I were getting the hang of it.

CHAPTER THIRTY-SIX

Make a Wish

Most people would be angry if an attendant even asked if they'd mind someone cutting in front of them when they've waited in line for 20-30 minutes under the scorching sun, but this was different. This was a child who was at Disney World as their "wish" with the Make-a-Wish Foundation. About 40% of the kids who make wishes make them for a vacation at Disney World, and some of them include week-long stays with their parents at the nearby Give Kids the World Village. I've volunteered at the Village, and so I'm also happy to see Make-a-Wish kids in line to see Pluto.

Some people, unfortunately, don't understand Make-a-Wish (or do understand, but just don't care). Their priority is to keep their place in line, no matter what. One day, in Magic Kingdom, Pluto saw an instance of people unwilling to let a little girl move ahead of them in line. The attendant had asked the family at the front of the queue if they'd let the Make-a-Wish girl get ahead of them. The mother rudely answered "no" in such a disgusted voice that you'd have thought the attendant had wanted to see her underwear. The second family in line parroted the first. Then came the third family:

Attendant: Would you mind if this young lady with Make-a-Wish went before you?

Mum and Dad: No, she can't; we've been waiting for ages.

Attendant: Do you know what Make-a-Wish Foundation does?

Dad: Yes, we do, but we've waited in line.

No attendant wants to get into an argument that will embarrass the Make-a-Wish family they're trying to help. Pluto was not impressed by the behavior and made no special effort with these families. He signed their books and posed for photos, but that was it. It wasn't in the character's nature to frolic with rude people. You'd think the first family in line would have gotten the message, but they might have emboldened by the others and they also refused to step aside. At that point, Pluto left his spot, took the hand of the Wish girl, and brought her forward. No one can argue with Pluto. He spent lots of time with this girl, who had waited so long and in much less comfort than the healthy people in front of her, and lined her and her family in front of the Castle and signaled to the PhotoPass photographer that she should take the shot with fireworks in the background. (The fireworks were at the end of the Dream Along with Mickey castle show, and they only go off twice at the end of the show; that's why Pluto had to be quick to make sure the family didn't miss them.)

I had the privilege to meet several other Wish kids on my program. By far, these encounters were among my favorites. I recall one in particular that happened in DinoLand during an 11-hour day. All the usual suspects were in the area: girls dressed as princesses, boys wearing the giant Goofy hats. Pluto saw a boy in a wheelchair stood near the exit with a purple Make-a-Wish button on his shirt. The attendant did his usual job of telling the family in line that a special guest was going to meet Pluto ahead of them, and they were happy to step aside. My partner for the day, Goofy, finished signing the autograph books of the Wish kid and his little sister, and then handed the books to Pluto. The boy enjoyed watching us sign the books, especially when Pluto did it, since Pluto puts autograph books on his snout to sign them. Surprising everyone, the boy said "thank you", the only words he'd spoken thus far (I got the impression that he doesn't speak much). He held out his hand and the attendant said: *"Pluto, he wants to hold your hand."*

With his other hand, the boy handed Pluto his hat and indicated with a thumbs-up that he wanted me to sign, which I did and then put it back on his head.

It was such a little thing, but it meant so much to the boy and his family, and it's why I wanted to be a performer in the first place.

CHAPTER THIRTY-SEVEN

Give Kids the World

"Let's go celebrate Christmas in July!"

This was one of the best experiences I had while working at Disney, and probably one of the best experiences of my life. As part of the College Program, you're given an events calendar when you arrive, and you can pick up a new one at the beginning of each month from the front desk of your housing complex. Every week through June there was a Give Kids the World event. I hadn't even read the calendar during my first program, but I'd heard people talking about it. I learned that Give Kids the World is held at a "village" where children with life-threatening illnesses and their families can enjoy a week's vacation. I wanted to do my bit and give what I could to help this worthy cause. Katie and I book our place on one of the upcoming event and were told to meet at the Commons that day at 4:30pm, where we would have a briefing, fill out some paperwork, and receive our volunteering t-shirts.

At the Commons, the event leader showed up with a armful of t-shirts and explained that she had only a limited supply of sizes. Luckily, Katie and I both got the size we wanted, and we put the shirts on right away over the strappy tops we were wearing.

We piled into the mini bus for the 20-minute drive from The Commons to the Village, where we handed in our registration forms and got our name stickers. We'd already been assigned a project. Today, as it turned out, was a particularly special day: it was a Thursday, and every Thursday the Village is turned into a Winter Wonderland, complete with a visit from Santa. It broke my heart when I realized that they were celebrating Christmas in July because some of these kids weren't going to make it to December.

We were taken to a volunteer hut and fed pizza, crisps, salad, brownies, and other treats, and told to help ourselves to a drink dispenser loaded with every kind of fizzy imaginable. Then we were taken to a laundry room where they'd hung rails full of glittery red, white, and green costumes. The leader began handing them out; there were elves, candy canes, Eskimos, presents, and tin men, all in a variety of sizes. I was given a fur blue dress with a hood lined with white fur. I thought I looked like a snow queen, but I was supposed to be an Eskimo. Katie was a candy cane in a red-and-white striped dress. We almost forgot it wasn't really Christmas time!

Now fully costumed, we were driven up the lane to where the parade would start. The parade was only a short route, but that didn't matter because when we got to the courtyard, there were Christmas themed decorations everywhere, and music playing. Two children (who had walked with me hand-in-hand during part of the parade) dragged me to the center and wanted to dance. As they laughed at my silly moves, a giant elf on stage with a microphone said that Santa had a special surprise for all the children staying here. The elf asked us all to close our eyes. At this point, I had been joined by a girl in her early teens wearing a bikini top and shorts, which revealed several scars across her stomach and rib cage. She had short hair which looked as if it had been recently shaved and was just now growing back. She looked at me and I indicated for her to close her eyes by covering mine with my hands. She grabbed my right hand and squeezed it with excitement as she closed her eyes. We all counted down from three and then opened our eyes to find that it was snowing. All the children were fascinated by the snow, and the teenager next to me had tears in her eyes. She gave me the biggest hug and ran off to find her parents.

Back home, I realize that I'd just gotten a huge wake-up call and needed to stop complaining about the trivial matters that I thought were so important, such as:

- Why does it matter if the makeup I like isn't in stock?
- Why does it matter if I'm not going to get a discount at my supermarket any more?
- Why does it matter if the top I want can't be shipped to the UK?

These are all things that I have complained about in the last month, and the kids I met at the Village put my attitude to shame.

CHAPTER THIRTY-EIGHT

A Guide to Meeting Characters at Disney

During my college program, I got pretty close to a few of the characters. I noticed a lot of things as a performer, and it only seems fair to share what I learned so that you'll have better luck when it comes your turn to meet Pluto and all of his friends.

- Be prepared. When the attendant says "get your pens, autograph books, and cameras ready", they mean it. Have them in your hands, ready to go.

- Have an itinerary. Know who in your group wants individual pictures and who just wants to be in the group picture. If you want individuals, decided whether it is really necessary for all 20 members of your group to have their own photos taken.

- Pens! Don't give the characters pens that are for meant for small, nimble fingers. Some of the characters have paws or big hands, and some are not able to pose their fingers. Mickey taught Pluto how to write especially so he could sign his name for guests, but please make it easy for him (and for characters like him) by giving him a big, thick, easily manipulated pen. I have seen Rafiki been forced to write with half a crayon, and on the other end of the scale, I've seen Pluto handed one of those giant novelty pencils. If you want a decent autograph, the character needs the right tool with which to give it to you.

- Sharpies. Be careful where you're pointing that thing. It's good that you uncap the pen to help out the character, but don't throw it at him or stab it into his palm nib-first. It's not easy to wash permanent marker out of fur.

- The characters do love to be hugged. But be gentle; a proper hug doesn't involve hanging off Rafiki's neck or using Pluto's nose as a pull-up bar. Some of the character performers are quite small and easily damaged.

- Mix things up a bit. The characters also know how to high-five and some can even fist bump. Some characters in the quieter meet-and-greet areas will even learn a new handshake if you want to teach them something cool. Pluto, in particular, loves learning new tricks, and for him a hand shake is definitely a trick.

- Talk to the characters. It's awkward if you just shove your paper at them expecting it to be signed without saying a word. You can even ask them questions and create a fun game of charades trying to guess their answer (for the ones unable to talk). It can be amusing to see how the character reacts when you guess wrong. Please do avoid stupid or intricate questions, however.

- Accept the PhotoPass card. You don't have to be rude to the photographer or attendant for asking you if you have or would like one. The cards are free, and you aren't bound into a contract to buy anything by accepting the card. The PhotoPass photographers are pros and will capture things on film that you're likely to miss.

- Character love presents, especially those handcrafted by children such as pictures, letters, stickers, origami, paper airplanes, bouncy balls, or anything small but memorable.

- Would you give your newborn baby to your dog at home? No! So don't give your newborn baby to Pluto. He sure doesn't want to hurt the little fella, but with big paws and fingers that don't always work so well, he does tend to drop stuff.

- Do not announce to the entire queue waiting to meet Mickey Mouse that he is "just someone in a costume". You may think you're cool or "above the magic" when you do this, but no one else will think so (if only you could hear what the people around you are likely thinking) and all you accomplish is to confuse the littler kids. Is that why you came to Disney World?

- Don't ask the characters, "Is it hot in there?" Of course it is, and that's why they're given frequent breaks. Also, see the previous comment, above.

- Think about what you are going to get signed. Hard book? Great! Tiny bits of paper made for ants? Not so great. Don't expect the best autograph ever if you just hand the character a loose sheet of paper. Pluto has an especially difficult time signing his name as his huge snout gets in the way, and he could use all the help you can give him.

- Bring fun things to sign. Signed t-shirts and even pillow cases make great souvenirs that cost you nothing. But again, remember to put something hard beneath that pillow case, or you'll be disappointed by the autograph. If you can't sign a t-shirt held in mid-air, neither can Pluto or any of the other characters. Bring a clipboard.

- And finally, if you are going to tell a character that they are your favorite and that you've watched all their TV shows and films, please get their name right. Pluto hates being called Goofy, especially when his name is right there on his collar.

CHAPTER THIRTY-NINE

The Famous Florida Thunderstorms

It was a DinoLand day, and I was at Animal Kingdom for 7am watching all of the breakfast workers coming out warm up as I was went into the base. The forecast today was for thunderstorms and torrential rain, with potentially a hurricane warning thrown in. This has always scared me. But the worst thing about today, besides the potential risk of a hurricane, was the likelihood of lightning, and my break room for the day was a caravan-type trailer. I was terrified that lightning would hit the trailer and kill us all.

We started the day as we usually did. I went out for my Pluto sets to meet the guests who were risking a day in the park despite the forecast. Around 11am, the heavens opened, with rain so heavy that we were told to report to our designated rain locations instead of our usual spots. But even getting to those locations would mean a lot of wet fur for Goofy and Pluto. Just as we were about to give it a try, the call came in: WE ARE 101!

The internal code 101 is used by cast members to report a location is no longer in use due to weather conditions or other issues. Usually, a weather-related 101 is linked to lightning, which means that the characters can't come out (they're too afraid) to play. Many of the rides shut down, as well. Disney foresaw the danger from lightning when they built the park, and if you look at the very top of Cinderella Castle you'll see a spire: that spire isn't for Cinderella to hang a washing line, it's a lightning conductor which is meant to redirect any errant bolt of lightning into the ground to discharge, with no harm to cast members or guests. Unfortunately, most of the other buildings don't have these lightning conductors, and so an electrical storm usually signals an unscheduled break for cast members (and an aggravation for guests).

Two hours into the 101 and it's still chucking down, and we were already through our first film in the trailer break room. As we started a vote as to what we would watch next, more lightning struck, followed by the loudest crack of thunder I'd ever heard.

Not even 10 seconds passed before the next bolt hit, seemingly right next to our trailer. I curled up on the sofa as the other girls screamed and the boys jumped out of their skins. Just as I was lifting my head up, another bolt hit. This one actually struck the trailer, causing it to shake. I vowed never to wish for another 101 ever again.

The insane weather conditions didn't stop before my shift ended, and so the van came to pick us and take us back to base. I always used to walk to the bus stop from base at animal kingdom, but today the weather was so bad that I had no intention of walking. I hid under the shelter and waited for the bus that went from the gates to base; it wasn't a very long trip, but it was far enough to get soaked. Unfortunately, on the other side of the gates there was another walk to the stop for the college program bus, but luck was finally on my side and the rain let up a little just as I went through the gates.

The bus was 30 minutes late, which wasn't unusual for a CP bus. We all queued up and proceeded to rush onto the bus to grab a seat. During the trip home, I looked at the many tourist hotels off Disney property and the tacky shops, including one with a giant eagle stuck on it. I guess the owner thought that a giant eagle would lure in tourists eager to buy his stupidly over-priced t-shirts, mugs, and key rings to prove to the folks back home that you'd had a wonderful time in Orlando.

We hadn't even reached the giant eagle before we were stuck in traffic caused by flooding. Our bus came to a halt just as thunder rumbled down once more. The storm grew worse as we sat there, not moving. I could feel tension building inside the bus. Everyone wanted to be home.

Finally, traffic began moving again, despite the thunder and lightning and sheets of rain. We drove through a "lake" that had been created in the middle of the road and then we were able to pick up a bit of speed. Almost immediately, however, a massive thunderclap shook the bus and lightning hit the road nearby. My phone rang at the same time, making me jump. It was Amy and Katie, advising me not to use my umbrella in these conditions.

Just then, another lightening bolt struck, only this time it didn't hit the road, it hit the back of the bus, causing a bang, screams, and sparks. The bus driver looked in his rear view mirror, and I could tell he was worried. I dropped my phone, ending my call to Amy and Katie, who undoubtedly had heard the loud bang and the dropped call and assumed that I might not be coming home, after all.

CHAPTER FORTY

Three Girls and Princess Dress Temptations

On the odd occasion when Katie and Amy and I would finish work at around the same time, we'd often head to Downtown Disney for an adventure, often involving Ghirardelli milkshakes. It was just as well that we didn't finish work at around the same time every day, because then I'd have needed to purchase an extra seat for the plane trip home. Each shake was a full day's caloric intake in a single glass, but so totally worth it.

Before we went to Ghirardelli's one night, we had a look around the shops. I had already begun making a list of the gifts I wanted to buy for people back home, and also the things I wanted to buy for myself before the program ended. One thing I wanted, but which I could never find in my size, was a princess dress. I had seen photos on Instagram of girls skinny as rakes fitting into the children's size princess dress, but that wasn't for me: at 5'7", it's safe to say that I'm not a stick. Katie and Amy, on the other hand, are so petite that they can get away with it.

Reluctantly, and with their urging, I picked up the largest princess dresses (a Rapunzel and a Merida) that I could find. It looked tiny. I sulked my way into the changing room, already jealous of Amy (who had found an Aurora and a Rapunzel in her size) and Katie (who had found an Ariel in hers).

With the expectation of having to pull off a skin-tight dress after struggling to get it on, I found to my surprise and delight that Rapunzel fit. (And yes, we still went to Ghirardelli's afterward...)

CHAPTER FORTY-ONE

Earning My Ears, Round Two

Graduation. Again. Last year, I excited to be chucking in my Housekeeping costume and getting on my flight home. This year, I was desperately trying to find a way not to leave.

I still had two weeks left in my program, but Disney had already set two dates for graduation. Everyone in my apartment managed to get one of those days off so we could attend the party and the ceremony together. Even the Americans, whose programs wouldn't end for another four months, decided to come along with us.

The festivities were to run from 10am–3pm, though few people stayed the entire time. It was more a drop-in affair. The ceremony was to be held on the Chatham Square field, within walking distance from our apartment, so we'd be spared a packed, sweaty bus ride.

Little was changed from last year, except for the people. We queued up for our graduation certificates and free photo frame boxes, then we got into another line for our Mickey ears, and then into still another line for a photo. From there it was all dancing, free food, and more lines for photos with the characters, including Pluto, who apparently had found another friend.

It was uncomfortably hot, as it always is in Florida during most of the summer, and so we cut things short and went back to the apartment to change into more comfortable clothes and spend the rest of the day in the Magic Kingdom, where we'd get our new ears hats embroidered.

Right away, we ran into the same problem as last year: the cast members who did the embroidering wouldn't do our hats because we weren't guests. Even though we'd worked here for months, practically for nothing, the company had decreed that we weren't worth a few strands of colorful thread. The rationale was that it wasn't fair for paying guests to have to wait in line while we had our hats done. I spoke to a manager about it, who was nice enough, but still wouldn't give in. I figured it was a cost issue, and so I offered to pay. No response. He didn't know what to say, because if we paid, then we'd be just like all the other guests standing in line. How could he refused that.

So we got in line, and I was quite happy to pay for the embroidery because it wasn't expensive. When got to the front and filled out the form, a lovely cast member who had been working in embroidery for years told us he had seen this same incident happen whenever there was a college program graduation. He felt it was foolish that some managers wouldn't graduates the simple courtesy of having their hard-won ears embroidered. Then he gave us a magic moment: we paid the basic price, but we didn't have to pay (as we normally would have) for an alternate color or font. It was a small but kind gesture, and we all appreciated it.

The four of us (myself, Amy, Katie, and our friend Greg) then walked to the top of Main Street to find a PhotoPass photographer to take a shot of us watching the Castle fireworks show. We wanted the photo to show our four names embroidered on the back of our hats. The photographer hurriedly sorted us into position by height, and then shouted: "3.....2....1......"

The fireworks went off. Our photo was perfect: it was the four of us looking up at the Castle with the fireworks positioned in the space to our left and right. A fitting end to this program.

CHAPTER FORTY-TWO

Season Finale

If my college program were an American TV show, then my last week would be considered the season finale. It brought many twists and turns.

On Wednesday, August 7, Molly rang Housing to report a leak in her and Courtney's bedroom. There had been yet another massive storm, and Molly discovered her bed was wet the day after. Many different members of the Housing team had appeared in the apartment to do assessments, but none led to a solution, and in the end they told us that we'd have to vacate the apartment because it had become unsafe. Our move-out date: Friday!

Since we were all still working, it was quite an effort to pack up everything and move it over to the new apartment, which luckily wasn't that far away. The effort seemed rather wasteful, as within a week I'd be leaving for home, so I unpacked in the new place very little of what I had packed in the old place. The best thing about the new apartment was its proximity to the vending machines, and we were also much closer to the bus stop.

But then the time had come: my final 24 hours as a cast member. I went one last time to the Magic Kingdom with Katie and Amy to watch the parade, have lunch, and pick up some last-minute souvenirs. Other friends joined us as the day wore on, and soon we were a group of seven. We chose a spot close to the Castle for the fireworks, but by this time our number had risen to fifteen, and so we were tightly packed. After the fireworks, we slowly walked out of the park.

I won't belabor again the teary goodbyes and farewells, since they were much the same as they were when my first program ended. It seemed unreal to wake up at 6am the following morning and realize that soon I'd be aboard a plane and that when the fireworks next shot over the Castle in the Magic Kingdom, I'd be an ocean away. As the Blue Fairy said at Wishes:

When stars are born, they possess a gift or two.

One of those is, they have the power to make a wish come true.

Chips vs Chips

Technically, we speak the same language, however, Americans and Brits have a linguistic barrier between them which resulting in others often giving me confused looks or asking, "Sorry, what did you say?"

This next story isn't intended to cause any offense, ; it's just a story I heard, not a story where I agree with the wording and how it's used.

A major mishap occurred in Magic Kingdom's Guest Relations. A British guest was waiting in line, packet of cigarettes in hand. When it came his turn to speak to the cast member behind the desk, he put his cigarettes in his pocket and asked, in language far too informal for the occasion: "Where can I go to have a fag?"

The cast member stared in shock. Trying to remain calm and polite, she replied: "I'm sorry, but you can't say that; it is not an acceptable way to talk about a person."

The guest turned red with embarrassment, realizing that no one in America calls cigarettes fags.

This story is just one of many. Once, when I came home from work, I had an encounter with Meritte, one of my American roommates, over the lack of cookies, snacks, and fizzy drinks in the apartment. I was upset at the thought of having to go to the shop, and so I had turned to Meritte and said I was "gutted". She looked at me and said, "What, like a fish?". Now, British people do say that you gut a fish, but we also say that we are gutted if we are upset about something.

On top of the confusion over word definitions, there are plenty of statements that we use but which Americans find funny. When I announced to my roommates that I was going to get some pudding before we started watching the next episode of whatever we were watching on TV, they were baffled by my sudden desire to eat pudding. What I meant was dessert.

Confused by British and American English? Here is a table of the words that got me the most odd looks at Disney World:

British	American
Half one (the time)	One thirty
Crisps	Chips
Chips	Fries
Bread Roll/Scone	Biscuit
Biscuit	Cookie
Waffle	Talks a lot
Rubbish	Garbage
Petrol	Gas
Sweets	Candy
Taxi	Cab
Wardrobe	Closet
Nappy	Diaper
Pram	Stroller
Motorway	Highway
Queue	Line
Trousers	Pants
Post	Mail
Pavement	Sidewalk
Trainers	Sneakers
Football	Soccer
Barmy	Crazy
Blatant	Obvious
Cheers/Ta	Thank you
Daft	Silly
Faff	Procrastinate
Fancy	Like
Gutted	Really upset
Kip	Nap
Porkies	Lies
Posh	High-class person
Busted	Broken
Plastered	Drunk

A Letter to Walt

Dear Walt,

First of all, thank you. These are the two most important words that I will ever need to say to you. Without you, I fear to think of what my life may have consisted of, and how incredibly boring film would be.

Disney has taught me about life, death, love, friendship, imagination, creativity, determination, and music. When I became old enough to apply for the Disney College Program, I was over the moon that I'd be able to work for your world not once but twice. I was even more appreciative of the cast members who work for your company and who hired me the second time around despite my inflexibility on a job role.

I will tell you one thing: Without the Disney College Program, I would never have learned how to cross an American road, which made me fear for my life. You should have warned everyone of these crazy crossroads that are near your world. American roads are weird, even when the man on the traffic light turns green, it doesn't mean that pedestrians can safely cross. You get a countdown timer, which panics me and makes me want to run, and the worst is if you get caught in the middle.

I would love for you to be able to clarify some myths, such as:

- Was Vista Way really donated by Coca-Cola?
- Where did the myth of your body being encased in ice and buried under the Pirates of the Caribbean ride come from?

I hope you are very proud of everything you achieved, because you are just one person, and you are proof that dreams really can come true. Not only did you make your dreams a reality, but your dream created dreams for millions of people across the world. I use your quotes on a regular basis, and I always thought that this book would be perfectly summed up with your "If you can dream it, you can do it!" but I found an even better one:

> You can dream, create, design, and build the most wonderful place in the world, but it requires people to make the dream a reality.

Sincerely,

Ema

Acknowledgments

This book wouldn't have been possible without:

- My mum and dad, for providing me with diet coke and brain food to fuel me through my book-writing hours;
- My brother, whose interest in Disney allowed me to use him as a test subject for much of this material;
- My boyfriend, and best friend, Glen, who let me to travel half-way across the globe, TWICE, to fulfill my dream of working for Disney; and
- My friends and fellow Cast Members: Amy, Abbie, Shauna, Katie, Courtney, Vicki, Molly, Christina, Meritte, Bethany, Ty, and Kevin.

And, of course, the Disney College Program itself wouldn't have been possible without Walt Disney and The Disney Company, who have created so many opportunities for so many people, and also the characters who have been and will always be some of my best friends.

About the Author

Ema Hutton recently completed a post-graduate certificate in Education at University of Central Lancashire, England. She hopes to return to work for the Disney Company at some point in the future. This is her first book.

About the Publisher

Theme Park Press is the largest independent publisher of Disney and Disney-related pop culture books in the world.

Established in November 2012 by Bob McLain, Theme Park Press has released best-selling print and digital books about such topics as Disney films and animation, the Disney theme parks, Disney historical and cultural studies, park touring guides, autobiographies, fiction, and more.

For more information, and a list of forthcoming titles, please visit:

ThemeParkPress.com

More Books from Theme Park Press

Amber Earns Her Ears

My Boss, Mickey Mouse

Come read Amber Sewell's Disney College Program diary and share her successes and her failures, her moments of delight and her moments of despair, and learn what happens when the pixie dust settles and the guests have gone home.

ThemeParkPress.com/books/ amber-earns-her-ears.htm

The Ride Delegate

Disney World for the 1%

The rich and famous experience Disney World differently from the rest of us: they're escorted by VIP Tour Guides, elite Cast Members who truly do hold the keys to the kingdom. Come meet the eccentric, outrageous guests who turned former VIP Tour Guide Annie Salisbury's life into a reality show.

ThemeParkPress.com/ books/ride-delegate.htm

More Books from Theme Park Press

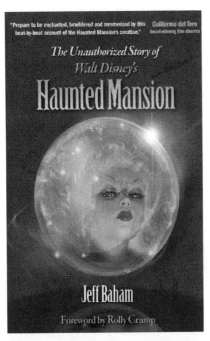

The Unauthorized Story of Walt Disney's Haunted Mansion

Welcome, Foolish Readers!

Haunted Mansion expert Jeff Baham recounts the colorful, chilling history of the Mansion and pulls back the shroud on its darkest secrets in this definitive book about Disney's most ghoulish attraction.

Foreword by Rolly Crump.

ThemePSarkPress.com/books/ haunted-mansion.htm

Murder in the Magic Kingdom

Who's Killing Walt Disney World Cast Members?

A body has turned up in the waters of the Jungle Cruise and Disney wants to pin the murder on Cast Member Josh Bates. With security closing in, Josh must race through the theme parks to solve the murderer's maddening riddles and clear his name.

ThemeParkPress.com/ books/murder-magic.htm

More Books from Theme Park Press

Two Girls and a Mouse Tale

Double Shot of the Disney College Program!

Two girls from Colorado spend a year in the College Program at Walt Disney World, balancing pixie dust with reality bites, as they spin magic for guests in the parks, but can't talk their roommates into keeping the apartment clean.

ThemeParkPress.com/books/two-girls-mouse-tale.htm

The Vault of Walt: Volume 3

Even More Unofficial Disney Stories Never Told!

Best-selling author Jim Korkis brings forth from his famous Vault of Walt two dozen new stories about Disney films and theme parks, Disney stars and attractions, and of course, Walt himself. Disney fans and historians alike will relish these little-known tales.

ThemeParkPress.com/books/vault-walt-3.htm

Discover our many other popular titles at:

www.ThemeParkPress.com

Printed in Great Britain
by Amazon

44219459R00079